Green Christmas

How to Have a Joyous, **Eco-Friendly** Holiday Season

Jennifer Basye Sander and Peter Sander

with Anne Basye

Aadamsmedia
Avon, Massachusetts

Published by
Adams Media, an F+W Publications Company
57 Littlefield Street, Avon, MA 02322. U.S.A.
www.adamsmedia.com

ISBN 10: 1-60550-041-0
ISBN 13: 978-1-60550-041-6

Printed in Canada.

J I H G F E D C B A

Library of Congress Cataloging-in-Publication Data
is available from the publisher.

This publication is designed to provide accurate and authoritative information with regard to the subject matter covered. It is sold with the understanding that the publisher is not engaged in rendering legal, accounting, or other professional advice. If legal advice or other expert assistance is required, the services of a competent professional person should be sought.

—From a *Declaration of Principles* jointly adopted by a Committee of the American Bar Association and a Committee of Publishers and Associations

Many of the designations used by manufacturers and sellers to distinguish their product are claimed as trademarks. Where those designations appear in this book and Adams Media was aware of a trademark claim, the designations have been printed with initial capital letters.

The pages of this book are printed on 100% post-consumer recycled paper.

This book is available at quantity discounts for bulk purchases.
For information, please call 1-800-289-0963.

Contents

1. Why Go Green for Christmas?

Christmas is a magical time of year. Close your eyes and think back on your best holiday memories. Chances are they don't have to do with elaborately wrapped gifts but instead involve moments of laughter at an old family joke, a snowy night of caroling with friends, or the sudden appearance of an unexpected friend. Wonderful moments of love, fellowship, and community.

Here's an idea: why not make this the year you give yourself the gift of enjoying a less stressful, less costly holiday season? One in which there are just as many, if not more, happy memories to treasure in the future. How is that possible? Simple—go green.

We promise you that, in the years to come, you won't look back on this holiday season, your first green Christmas, and wish you'd gone to the mall more often, spent more lavishly, and left the lights on all night long. Whenever you waver in your resolve to cut back on the lavish and focus on the simple this season, go back to those same warm memories of Christmas Past. They'll remind you why you're making a change.

This book is an invitation to join us in going green this holiday and beyond. It's the perfect time to begin living more lightly on planet Earth. The traditional concept of Christmas as a season of love and reflection fits in beautifully with your desire to help the world by making changes in your lifestyle. Many churches and faith-based groups are making protecting the environment a part of their year-round message, and this past spring the pope added destroying the environment to his list of sins. Adopting the simple green mantra of "give more, consume less" is a Christmas gift we can give to future generations. Give more of yourself and less of what's wasteful.

A real change is afoot, and many Americans are already eco-inclined, able to see that for the health of the planet we must make changes in the way we think and live. Peter and Jennifer Sander and Anne Basye lead lives that are probably a lot like yours. Peter and Jennifer are trying to raise a couple of happy and healthy young boys in a somewhat suburban setting in a pretty ordinary town. We don't live on a commune, our house isn't built from nontoxic materials, and we aren't raising all of our own food. As a family though, we are trying to do a better job of being citizens of this planet. We aren't green experts by any means (although come to think of it Peter was in charge of the campus recycling program in high school), we are ordinary Americans who know we all need to start making changes, both big and small, in the way we live so that our children, and their children, can continue to enjoy the beautiful world around us.

Peter and Jennifer have always been a frugal pair. We try to ignore the constant advertising drumbeat and instead focus on only buying things that we truly need, rather than what we (or our two young boys) want. We look around the house continually to consider what we can reuse, repurpose, or recycle.

Of the two sisters behind this book, Jennifer and Anne, Anne is even more frugal. She lives in a conventional building in a big city—Chicago—but does her best for the planet by not owning a car, recycling everything, and buying very little that is new. At Christmas, she favors recycled Christmas trees. (Read more about that in Chapter 5.)

Anne's son Alex is in his twenties, well beyond his rush-to-the-Christmas-stocking years. Where Jennifer and Peter have the expertise on nuclear family holidays, empty-nester Anne is an expert on friends-and-extended-family Christmases. Her presents and parties are for grownups.

This book is stuffed full of holiday-themed ideas on how to live lightly on the planet by making your own gifts and cards, wrapping presents in eco-friendly ways, and entertaining without waste. To get your family to join in willingly, you can also bring those things up at the table and let everyone toss out their own creative ideas on how to use (or reuse) what you have.

Some of the ideas will seem familiar. Why? Because a lot of green ideas are just basic good neighborly ways to behave. Rideshare to a holiday party? Sure, you do that anyway. It's called a designated driver! Offer to swap party clothes with a girlfriend instead of buying new things? It's called friendship, and you do it all the time.

Changing Your View

"What is Christmas all about?" This is a perennial topic in women's magazines and inspirational editorials. Every year we are exhorted to remember the reason for the season—and then we forget, buckling under pressures to conform.

The cost of conforming in the United States is great. Every year between Thanksgiving and New Year's Day, Americans generate 25 million extra tons of garbage (about 25 percent more than during the rest of the year) and spend billions of dollars on purchases that may trigger an uptick on Wall Street but leave consumers burdened with more debt.

Cramming too many events into too few days is another cost of conforming. You know what it feels like to be so overextended and tired that it's hard to enjoy the holidays. Conforming to a conventional Christmas harms you and harms the earth. To explain why, let's take a moment to examine global warming.

A Short Overview of Climate Change

As we were writing this book, Anne heard a meteorologist and an attorney for the Natural Resources Defense Council present a really great overview of global warming. The weatherman, an old pro at making complicated weather phenomena comprehensible to the average television viewer, explained that *climate* refers to the long-term average weather conditions of a region, while *weather* refers to the state of the atmosphere at a specific time in a specific place.

The topic of climate change puts most of us to sleep, he acknowledged, because it involves long-term statis-

 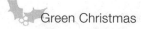

tics and scientific models that can be tough to follow. The topic of *climate variability*, on the other hand, is easier to understand because we can see it. When tornadoes strike when there is snow on the ground, or it's 65 degrees in January, we know that something's wrong with climate variability.

The fact that the climate is changing is indisputable. The reasons for that change are what people argue about. So if someone in your life is skeptical about "global warming" and scoffs at your green measures, let them know that scientists agree that there is a 90 percent chance that heat-trapping pollution has been the main factor behind the gradual warming of the planet since 1950. Check the sidebar above, and you'll see that the warmest years of the last century almost all fell in the last ten years.

Why? Every year humans emit 7 billion tons of carbon dioxide. The oceans, trees, and other natural processes of the earth can only absorb about 3 billion tons annually. That means that every year we emit 4 billion tons of CO_2 too many. That leads to a concentration of CO_2 in the atmosphere, which sets in motion a process that traps the heat, warms the planet, and is threatening to turn northern Illinois, where Anne lives, into West Texas by the end of the twenty-first century.

Day in, day out, whether it's Christmas or not, Americans, per capita, emit more CO_2 than anybody else on the planet. For planet temperatures to stabilize, the world needs to cut emissions by 50 percent—but we Americans need to cut back between 60 and 80 percent.

Through a combination of energy conservation and energy efficiency, it *can* be done. We've already made some great strides. Over the past thirty or so years, our economy has grown steadily more energy efficient. Smaller cars, better insulation in buildings, more efficient heating and cooling technologies . . . all these things have made it possible to enhance our lifestyles while using less energy. Unfortunately, the new ways we have dreamed up to consume energy have nearly canceled that savings. So while we now can make refrigerators bigger and many times more energy efficient than they were thirty years ago, we now drive farther and have many more energy-eating devices to power.

Goodbye, White Christmas?

Because of our CO_2 emissions, the global ice cap has shrunk by 40 percent since 1979. The water level of the Great Lakes, where Anne lives, could lower by four to five feet, according to the U.S. Environmental Protection Agency. And someday, in her part of the world, there will be no more snow. Already, the local forest preserve toboggan slopes, beloved by three generations of Chicagoans, have closed. The cost of making snow may bankrupt the little family-owned ski resort just across the border in Wisconsin where Anne and her son ski.

Going green—changing our personal energy consumption patterns—could help turn the tide. Preserving a White Christmas is certainly one reason to consider celebrating a green Christmas. But there are deeper reasons. If Christmas is at least partially about showing family and friends how much we care for them, isn't the best gift we could give the commitment to reducing our carbon load? Instead of celebrating in ways that ignore the planet—the planet where our loved ones live—shouldn't we start figuring out creative new ways to live, love, and celebrate that mean just as much but cost the earth less?

The December holidays bring out our creativity in the presents we make, the meals we cook, and the rituals we enact. So why not learn a few new creative

Christmas habits that can become year-round practices to benefit our climate? This could be the year that you think outside the Christmas box and create a more joyful, eco-friendly, low-stress holiday for yourself and everyone around you!

Get the Family Involved Early

Deciding to go green for the holidays should involve your whole family. Not everyone will understand, of course, and you need to be prepared for that. Some will cling desperately to their old notions of what the traditional holiday season is about and how we should all behave, but change is good, and good change is even better!

A great way to get started on your green holiday is to make it a topic of conversation at the Thanksgiving dinner table. Gathered around the table that afternoon will be most of the people with whom you usually celebrate Christmas: the children who hope for mounds of gifts wrapped in shiny paper under a tree hung heavy with tinsel, the grandparents who enjoy indulging their grandchildren, and the spouse who has been flipping through catalogs for months, folding down the corners to mark various gift ideas. Will this group warmly embrace the idea of giving more by consuming less? You'd be surprised. You might find that everyone else seated around the table has had the exact same thought. Here are a few topics to discuss at the dinner table:

- Is there a way we can try to cut back on energy consumption this year?
- Can we work on reducing our waste during this holiday season?
- What if we scaled back the gift giving and focused on experiences and good times with each other?

Some of the loved ones who gather may be reluctant to probe these questions or entertain changes to your family's cherished traditions. (Parents of small children are different—you'll have special challenges, but after all, you're in charge!) Especially if your clan is a large one, there will be many opinions. Your questions may appear to threaten shared rituals or come too late for people who finished their shopping in October, but at least a few of those gathered will be ready to consider green holiday alternatives. Perhaps those few can take the first steps this Christmas and inspire more to join in next year.

Make Your Goals Green?

Ask yourself and your family what would be a reasonable goal to achieve together. No sense loudly declaring that you will all go 100 percent green this Christmas and vow to spend only twenty dollars total. It's a bit like dieting or any other major resolution—the minute you stray a bit off the path you get discouraged and junk the whole plan. Instead, choose a number that you might be able to beat. Maybe you could try to be just 20 percent greener this holiday season, and, hey, you might end up at 30 percent! You know what? That would be a major accomplishment. If a bunch of us around the country could end up being 30 percent greener this Christmas it would make a big impact. More could join in, and more, and think of what we could accomplish together!

A More Joyous Time of Year

A whopping 75–90 percent of people report that they feel down during the holidays. Maybe they feel lonely or stressed about money. This is a time of year when so many of us look around and decide that in many ways we don't measure up to some standard we're told about—or that we imagine. You might think that your family doesn't look like those bright and shiny people in the holiday commercials. Maybe your body doesn't look like the beautifully dressed bodies in the ads, or your income isn't adequate for the products on display. How much easier it would be to ignore these messages.

Here's a great way to refocus. Draw up a list of the things you don't enjoy during the holidays. Is it seeing a relative who makes you feel bad about yourself? Having the same argument with your spouse about how much you can afford to spend? Worrying about how long it will take to pay off the credit cards?

Now draw up a list of things that you enjoy about the holidays, for example, visiting with friends you hardly ever see, reading a Christmas letter from an old college pal, or welcoming a group of friends and family into your home. Is there a way you can do much more of the second list and less of the first? We're sure there is, and in the chapters to come you will find many ideas to help you achieve that goal while going green. Join in, and together let's make this the greenest Christmas ever.

Green Christmas FAQs

Won't my children hate this?
Actually, young children are really aware of what is happening to our environment. Not only do they hear about it all the time in school and on television, global warming is also a fast-growing category of science projects. They will love getting involved with your efforts

to do something cool like cut back on waste and use less stuff, especially if your family experiment helps get that science project done!

Isn't all that green stuff more expensive?
One of the basic tenets of living lightly is to consume less. When you are consuming less, you will buy fewer things. If it costs a tad more to buy a nontoxic cleaner, you will be able to afford it! The more popular green products become, the more affordable they will become. And with today's higher energy costs, they're becoming more affordable than ever.

Will my friends think I'm a Scrooge?
Some might, but others will secretly be thrilled that you are leading the way on this issue. They've been meaning to do it themselves! You'll become a role model.

What if I end up blowing it and never do a green thing?
Try again on December 26, then on December 27. Hey, we all know Al Gore lives in a really big house, so none of us is perfect. Just keep trying.

Will any of this make a difference?
Yes. Yes. Yes. Every action, both big and small, makes a difference. Not just for what you and your family do

today, but for the message and lifestyle impression you make on your children and others around you.

Doesn't the economy depend on me going to the mall?
The great thing about American business is that it adapts quickly. Buy green, and it will produce green and sell green in that mall. Buy American green, and there will be green American jobs.

Will it really feel like Christmas if I do things differently?
This is your chance to develop more meaningful traditions that give you the sense of creating your own personal holiday rather than going along with commercialism.

Isn't it time-consuming to go green?
In some ways it can be, if you're building a building or making dramatic changes in the way you commute. When it comes to Christmas, by incorporating some of these ideas, you'll have more free time because you won't be caught up in the frenzy of consumption. Sure, it can be tempting to lapse into our usual drive-through, take out, and convenient choices, but convenience takes its ecological toll. Just like cooking a great meal takes a little more thought and planning, living green takes some upfront thought. Do it once, and it will become the natural way of doing things—cheaper, easier, better.

2. The Holiday Environment

Clean air, clean water. That used to be the definition of a "clean" environment. Today it's gotten complicated. Sure, clean air and clean water are among the most important results of environmental sensitivity, but to focus directly on air and water would miss the point. We need to look closely at the causes of dirty air and dirty water, because that's where most of the solutions lie.

Those causes can be grouped into three categories:

- *Waste*—solid and liquid refuse we can all see, touch, and smell
- *Emissions*—gaseous refuse we can sometimes smell (oh, can we ever?!) and sometimes not even detect, like carbon dioxide (CO_2)
- *Energy*—the stuff we use to drive our cars, heat our homes, and power all manner of things, including the factories that make the objects we use

Energy results directly in emissions, but it also causes a lot of environmental headaches in its production and distribution.

What do the environment and holidays have in common? Why would the environment be any different during the holidays than at any other time of the year? Because we ramp up. We increase energy use, waste, and emissions directly and indirectly through the consumption of more and more.

Christmas is the season of love, the season of giving, but, sadly, it is also the season of waste. You just read in the first chapter that every year during the holidays Americans produce many, many extra tons of trash.

How much extra trash? Remember that big statistic from Chapter 1—our household waste increases 25 percent from Thanksgiving to New Year's, adding some 1 million tons per week to our landfills. The U.S. Environmental Protection Agency (EPA) keeps track of these kinds of things. That's not all we do while celebrating either. We use a lot more energy to heat our homes, travel, and decorate for the holidays. Christmas lights alone, especially those good old-fashioned incandescent bulbs, can use hundreds of kilowatt-hours (kWh) per household.

And what about holiday travel? Do we ever travel! The American Automobile Association estimates that some 65.2 million Americans drive more than fifty miles to a holiday destination. That doesn't include miles traveled for routine friends and family visits during the season, and it also doesn't include the 9 million or so who travel by air. Despite higher gas prices, the number of people traveling by car has increased every year. Speaking of gas, according to the authors of *Use Less Stuff*, if each family saved one gallon of gas during the holidays, that would result in some 1 million fewer tons of CO_2 in the atmosphere.

So before we get to the fun stuff about decorating your house and giving green gifts to our loved ones, let's get serious and talk about waste. Let's talk about energy. Let's talk about emissions. And let's talk some more about travel (which we will in Chapter 7—Green Holiday Getaways).

Waste Not, Want Not

An extra million tons of trash into the landfills a week? Ewww . . . how do we do that? Well, think about it— much of celebrating Christmas has to do with paper. Wrapped gifts, holiday cards, packaging materials, boxes of all sizes and shapes, newspaper advertising

> ### RECYCLE, RECYCLE, RECYCLE!
> According to Fridey Cordingley, head of a U.K. group called Recycle Now, "41 percent of people say they let their good intentions lapse over Christmas but . . . recycling is one of the easiest things you can do to help."

inserts, catalogs, little green cocktail napkins—the list of paper goods goes on and on.

Let's start with holiday cards. According to Hallmark, the 1.9 billion Christmas cards sold each year in the United States could fill a football field ten stories high and consume 300,000 trees. How about this—if we send one card less per family, we'd save some 50,000 cubic yards of paper. E-cards would easily make a big difference here. Maybe the good news is that handwritten thank-you notes don't add much to the waste stream as we all know they never really get written.

It isn't just paper either. Bet you never thought about food waste, right? Another fact from *Use Less Stuff* is that some 28 billion pounds of food are wasted each year— some 100 pounds per person. And we know a lot of that happens during the holidays. Think about this—if every American threw away just one uneaten tablespoon of mashed potatoes, that would add 16 million pounds of waste to our landfills. We don't know who has the time to research these things, but they must have been eating the mashed potatoes at the same dinner party we went to.

You might hang your green felt hat on recycling, and indeed recycling programs have had their impact, particularly on things like newspapers, aluminum cans, and beverage bottles. At one time, most of the Christmas trees sold each year end up in a landfill, but more recent statistics show that today some 93 percent of all live trees are recycled in some form of community program. The news on plastics and other materials is more mixed: while we do recycle some 25 percent of those plastic soda bottles, only 3.9 percent of postconsumer plastic is recycled in total. And of all the 100 billion plastic grocery sacks produced a year, only 2 percent are recycled. There is room for improvement here, wouldn't you agree?

Nuts to Packing with This Stuff!

What about those danged packing peanuts (the ones that fall out all over your living room floor when you open the package from your Aunt Mary)? You can reuse them yourself, put them into the next box you send out, and encourage the next person you send them to also reuse rather than toss them in the trash. Or you can give them to a packing store or your local UPS or FedEx folks to reuse. Whatever you choose will be better than sending them to a landfill for the next thousand years or so.

Christmas catalogs, dozens and dozens of them, arrive daily from September on. Is there a way to cut down the onslaught a bit and get off of these bleeping lists? Yes. Check out *www.catalogchoice.org*. It's free to sign up, and the site lets you opt in for the catalogs you want. Once you do that, those catalogs will be the only ones you get, not the pesky ones you never asked for. Instead of you contacting every company that you don't want to hear from, these folks will do it for you.

The Direct Marketing Association, an industry trade group of catalog and direct marketers, offers a similar service known as DMA Choice. It isn't free to sign up—it costs a buck for a processing fee—but DMA works with catalog marketers to figure out who really does and who doesn't want catalogs. Your catalog choices turn into useful information for other marketers too. Use one of these two services, and you're likely to dramatically reduce the mail in your mailbox during the fall season.

What is the potential impact of large numbers of people opting off of catalog lists? Catalogs are estimated to consume some 8 million trees each year, not to mention the carbon footprint of all that paper processing, mail distribution, and, well, that eventual trip to the recycling center or landfill. If retailers have fewer places to send their catalogs, they'll print fewer catalogs.

Recycle Today for Tomorrow

Yes, you recycle. Of course you do. Recycling really kicks in as a green move when the recycled material is used to produce something else, thereby eliminating the need to produce more glass, paper, and so forth. So it is extremely important to close the loop and also buy things that are made out of recycled materials. All kinds of cool things are made from other things nowadays.

There's a company called Trex that makes composite outdoor deck material out of recycled plastic grocery bags. Trex reportedly buys more than half the grocery bags that come through the recycling process. Most of you won't be putting new decks on your homes during the holidays, but it's still good to understand the model.

There are many small gift items made from post-consumer recycled waste. From an online store called Real Green Goods (*www.realgreengoods.com*), check out:

- The doorstop made from scrap bits of fine hardwood
- The sun catcher kaleidoscope, and the coaster sets made from recycled glass
- The bracelets made from recycled beads

Look in our shopping chapter for many more sources of gifts and products made from recycled materials.

This Christmas season why not commit to seeking out gifts made from recycled materials? Or maybe plan to buy at least half of your gifts made from recycled materials? Any step in that direction is a good one. Why? Because it expands the market for recycled materials, and it brings awareness to the gift recipient—if they aren't aware already!

Keep a Green Logbook

Being green isn't just about what you buy for others. It's about what you use yourself, too. Here's an idea: start a Green Logbook. Write down what you consume and throw away every day the same way dieters record what they eat every day in an effort to cut back. You can even save paper and put your logbook online with a green blog in order to share what you've learned.

Keeping track for just a few days will open your eyes to the amazing amounts of garbage produced in our daily lives. You'll become more focused on how your actions affect the health of the planet. Soon you'll find yourself making different decisions throughout the day. *Hey, that piece of paper I was about to toss, can I turn it over and use the backside? Maybe my morning shower could be shorter; I'll save water and get to work on time! Wonder if my next-door neighbor also needs to go to the grocery store this afternoon and wants to rideshare?*

Not surprisingly, the holidays will be one of the more revealing times to keep track of waste, just as it's a pretty good time to track those calories!

Avoid the Nonrecyclables

Sometimes it's hard to know what is and what isn't recyclable. Soda cans, bottles, and newspapers? Sure. But what about other stuff? Items crafted of blended materials like glitter cards or foil wrap present special problems for recyclers. And those mostly plastic electronic toys present challenges for recyclers too—most can't be recycled. Think about the box they're packaged in. Many of the boxes have a mix of paper and cellophane or plastic. The paper itself and the ink on it make the recycling process difficult. Add the plastic window and the foam or Styrofoam inside, and you have a mess.

The 1.9 billion holiday cards are a good place to start. There are lots of cards made out of recycled materials, and—you guessed it—if it's made of recycled materials, it can be recycled. Look for the recycled content label on the back of the card. It should tell you the percentage of PCW—postconsumer waste—used in the card. Here are some other green approaches:

- Check out card sellers like *www.paporganics.com*. Paporganics and others have cards made from tree-free fibers like hemp or bamboo.
- Send a greeting with one of the e-cards available at *www.threeleafcards.com*. At Three Leaf Cards you pay a one-time membership fee that lets you send an unlimited number of specially designed video cards. Their holiday cards have short videos and music; you can send someone a moving violin piece with a sweet picture of a shaggy dog in front

of a Christmas tree and a flickering (yes, it really flickers) fire.

- Pick up the phone to give someone a holiday call. After all, isn't that a better way to really connect and let someone know you are thinking about her or him?

REMIND OTHERS TO RECYCLE

Add a message to your cards this year encouraging folks to reuse them. A gift tag, a post card, a tree decoration, a bookmark—use anything to give that card a second life. Remember not to write the recycling message on an extra piece of paper!

What other kinds of things can you keep out of the trash? Always be on the lookout for ways to reuse and recycle. A wonderful British Web site called How Can I Recycle This?, *www.recyclethis.co.uk*, has 500 alternatives to pitching things in the trash. The magazine *ReadyMade* is filled with ideas on how to turn an old thing into a new thing. They now have their entire edition online at *www.readymademag.com*.

Planning to serve box wines to your guests? Those plastic bladders inside the box, together with the cardboard, are an almost impossible combination to recycle. Also, the type of plastic used will almost guarantee survival into many future millennia. They're airtight and watertight, so one clever reader of How Can I Recycle This? suggested ripping out the bladders, filling them with air, and using them for packing material—for next year's gift shipment or whatever you'd like. There are a lot more ideas where this one came from, and they're discussed in Chapter 8. You'll find great ways to recycle and reuse your way to holiday gift giving. Check it out.

Slash Those Emissions

Chapter 1 touched briefly on the onerous situation of emissions, most particularly those of the carbon dioxide (CO_2) variety, but there are many other kinds of emissions. No, CO_2 won't kill you, but some of the other bad stuff that are combustion byproducts certainly could!

What is a winter night without a cozy fire burning in the hearth, the sound of logs crackling and snapping, and the faint aroma of wood smoke? Sadly, just like the fact that our devotion to summertime outdoor charcoal grilling turns out to be not so green, wood smoke puffing out of your chimney isn't the greatest thing for the environment either. Recent studies have declared that smoke from wood fires is as bad or worse than smoke from cigarettes. It's filled with minute particles that can cause asthma and bronchitis, as well as other heart and lung diseases. It delivers a cocktail of aromatic hydrocarbons, formaldehyde, and benzene with a certain amount of carbon monoxide—just like cigarette smoke.

Some communities are actually limiting the number of days their residents can burn wood in their fireplaces.

Many California towns, like Sacramento, near Jennifer and Peter's home, restrict residents' choice to have a wood fire on nights when air quality is bad. If your area is like this, please abide by the restrictions.

Build a Cozy Fire

Strange as it may seem, the greener choice in wood fires then is to *not* burn actual wood logs! One choice is to burn fire logs made from recycled materials.

What's better than cozying up to a glowing fire? Cozying up to an environmentally friendly fire! Duraflame has developed a nonpetroleum fire log made from completely renewable resources such as recycled wood fibers and biowaxes derived from organic materials. Cleaner burning than wood fires, these fire logs produce 80 percent fewer emissions than a regular wood fire. No newcomer to recycling, Duraflame was started in the 1960s to recycle wood waste from a family pencil business (now there's a smart recycling application!). Every year the company recycles about 50,000 tons of wood chips and sawdust and saves 1.2 million trees from use as firewood. Their products or similar products—can be easily found in your local grocery store. Incidentally, the Duraflame Web site (*www.duraflame .com*) takes you on a nice tour of their approach to environmental issues.

How about a log made from coffee grounds? Good idea! Save those grounds from their inevitable trip to the landfill and put the subtle aroma of coffee into your living room and neighborhood. Java Products Company (*www.java-log.com*) makes a Java-Log—a fire log made from used coffee grounds. This Canadian-made product produces 79 percent less particulate material and 78 percent less carbon monoxide than natural firewood. You can find them at Whole Foods.

Get Some Winter Exercise

This one's kind of obvious, but if you shovel your own snow instead of using a snowblower, you'll reduce emissions. Snowblowers are like lawnmowers, and the total emissions from lawnmowers and leafblowers has caused a lot of concern. There isn't much reason to talk about lawnmowers in a Christmas book, but according to the EPA, a push mower powered by a gasoline motor gives off as much pollution per hour as eleven cars, and a riding mower emits as much per hour as thirty-four cars.

Many models of lawnmowers and snowblowers emit considerable quantities of carbon monoxide and nitrous oxides. And what better place to find out how much your snowblower emits than to look north of the border—at Environment Canada's snowblower emission calculator at *www.etc-cte.ec.gc.ca/databases/ SnowblowerEmissions/Default.aspx.*

So grab a shovel, clear off your walkway, and work off some of those extra Christmas pounds.

Become an Energy Star

We've all become aware of the rising costs of energy in both dollar and environmental terms. There is no need to repeat it all here, but there is a lot you can do during the holidays—and then all year round—to cut the size of your energy footprint.

Lighting Up the Christmas Night

We think most of you would agree that, regardless of your family traditions and religious feelings about the winter holidays, the tradition of Christmas lights is a favorite. Colorful, festive, and creative, they light the night at an otherwise pretty dark and gloomy time of year. But those lights—well—the technology first appeared in 1882 when Edward Johnson, an associate of Thomas Edison, created the first string of Christmas lights. President Grover Cleveland lit the first White House tree in 1095, and the tradition has been with us ever since. They haven't changed much since then, so they're due for a pretty serious update. Those regular incandescent bulbs we're all familiar with consume from 4 to 10 watts each.

At the national average electric rate of 10.4 cents per kilowatt-hour, a 10 watt bulb running for a hundred hours uses a penny's worth of electricity, but if you have 500 or 1,000 bulbs on your house, it can add up quickly. The latter half of the twentieth century did bring us those familiar little "mini" bulbs that use only 0.4 watts apiece, which is pretty tiny, but taken all together, thousands of lights times thousands of homes adds up to a pretty big number.

LEDs (light-emitting diodes, for you techie types) are used in traffic signals (those little colored dots) and on many newer car tail lights. While traditional light bulbs generate more heat than light (90 percent of the energy goes into heat), LEDs burn clean and bright. They consume about 80 percent less energy than regular incandescents and last a long time. LED Christmas lights are estimated to last 50,000 hours, which translates to eight hours a day for seventeen *years*.

The creative application of LEDs has just begun. In 2007, for the first time the giant Christmas tree at Rockefeller Center was decorated with LED lights. The upfront cost is still high but will come down dramatically as they

MODERN-DAY WRINGER WASHER

Almost any appliance has an off-the-grid version. You can find them at Lehman's (*www.lehmans.com*), which offers cool stuff like a small, nonelectric hand-washing machine and hand-cranked flashlights. Try a composter made from recycled plastics. There are lots of good gift ideas—for others and for yourself.

become more popular. You can get new strings of LED lights or find retrofit bulbs for your existing strings.

- A company called Christmas Lights and Decorations (*www.christmaslightsanddecorations.com*) is a good place to start as they provide plenty of educational material about new kinds of Christmas lights and decorations and offer plenty of choices for sale.
- Another good source is Christmas Lights Etc. (*www .christmaslightsetc.com*). They let you choose individual LED bulb styles in packs of twenty-five or more and sell empty strings to build your own set. Of course, you can buy the bulbs only to retrofit your old strings. A set of twenty-five size C7 outdoor bulbs costs about $36 (just under $1.50 each), and the string costs $6.50.
- Solar Illuminations (*www.solarilluminations.com*) sells strings of solar-powered holiday lights starting at about $40 per string of fifty LEDs. Again, it's not cheap yet, but we know where this is going.

Calculate Your Carbon Footprint

Reducing emissions is a nice idea, but except for that fireplace smoke, it's hard to see the result! If you decide to shrink that size 13 carbon footprint into little green elf booties this holiday, there are ways to see where you are.

We recommend two Web sites to calculate your carbon emissions: one at a site called LiveNeutral (*www.liveneutral.org*) and another—of all places—at BP, the big oil company. Check out this really good one at *www.bp.com* in their "Environment and society" page. The BP site lets you answer a few questions about the size of the house you live in, the type of car you drive, and your travel habits, and then it calculates your total carbon footprint. Jennifer learned that her 15 tons a year is lower than the average of 18.58 for our country. On the LiveNeutral site you can get specific details for your cars. There Jennifer punched in the info on her Volvo and learned that it produces 9,312 pounds of CO_2 annually. The LiveNeutral site will also sell you a carbon offset to neutralize your impact. Jennifer's Volvo would cost $33.75 to neutralize.

Whatever does that mean? When you buy a carbon neutral certificate from LiveNeutral, they buy third-party-verified and legally accountable emissions reduction credits from the Chicago Climate Exchange (CCX). These reduction credits then function as the offset for your emissions. Incidentally, measuring your carbon footprint can lead to some pretty nice New Year's goals and resolutions.

Water, Water, Everywhere

Do we use more water at holiday time? Christmas is not a big water-focused holiday, unless you think about adding water to your tree on a regular basis. Yet the holidays are a good time to focus on how much water we use in our ordinary lives.

We've all experienced energy shortages, electricity shortages, and shortages of everyday staples like coffee and cheap airplane seats. How long has it been since you thought about the abundance of water? Turn the tap on and out it comes, any day, any time, no matter what. That may be all about to change.

If you live in the desert or in one of the many communities supported by the Colorado River in the Southwest, you know what we're talking about. If you lived in the humid subtropical climate of Georgia in 2007, you also learned because it wasn't very subtropical that year.

But there's a bigger problem. Nationally, our aquifers (those zones into which we put wells) are dropping. So there's less to be had in places like Denver or Dallas. Globally, the situation is the same. Water covers two-thirds of the earth, but we humans have access to less than 0.8 percent, and we use most of it for agriculture. Two-thirds of the global population is expected to live in water-stressed conditions over the next twenty-five years. For most of them, that will mean no access to clean, safe water—or political conflicts based on who gets what. Worse, the so-called water infrastructure is crumbling. You see, most of it was put into the ground as big honkin' iron pipes over a hundred years ago. Know what happens to one-hundred-year-old iron pipes? You can imagine.

As if that wasn't enough, water is heavy, and it takes a lot of energy to move around. It must be pumped out of the ground and through all those pipes to bring it into your home. Even if fed by gravity from one of those cool "lollipop" water towers, it has to get *into* the tower somehow. And the bottled stuff? That brings another set of problems.

Cut Out the Bottled Water Hazard

The environmental issues with the pumping, pro-duction, and delivery of ordinary tap water pale in comparison to those associated with its plastic-bottled cousins. Those plastic bottles must be manufactured. Then, copious amounts of energy are used to haul it around in trucks—far more than to pump it through pipelines.

According to the Earth Policy Institute, some 8 billion gallons of bottled water are consumed annually—8 ounces per person per day. Making the plastic for those bottles consumes some 1.5 million barrels of oil, enough to power 100,000 cars for a year. Only about 10 percent of that material is recycled, as much of it flies under the radar of state recycling programs. Peter Gleick, of the Oakland-based Pacific Institute, estimates that all activities involved in producing and delivering a bottle of water would consume enough energy to fill a quarter of the bottle with oil.

As it becomes more widely known that most bottled water originates from municipal water sources (both Coke and Pepsi recently acknowledged as much), and as experts from research scientists to Berkeley's famed Chez Panisse restaurant have publicly favored tap water over the bottled stuff, think about doing the same for yourself. Guess what—you'll save a lot of money too, because the markup on a bottle of water ranges from 250 to 10,000 percent! Even at today's prices, a gallon of gas costs about a third of the cost of a bottle of water. You'll also help reduce waste. Water bottles are the fastest-growing form of municipal waste in the United States. By choosing to avoid water bottles you can help slow that alarming trend.

On the green side, some large retailers, including Wal-Mart and Kroger's, have announced that they are selling water in thinner bottles that use less plastic. To be truly green, skip the bottled water.

Saving Water

Other than skipping the bottled water, what are some ways to cut back on ordinary water use during the holidays? Here's a real simple green water-recycling habit to adopt for Christmas. Save the water from the kitchen (water that you boiled pasta in, cooked veggies with, or rinsed off fruit) and, once it cools, add it to the Christmas tree water to keep it fresh. A small gesture, yes, but it's one that will help you stop and focus for a moment on how much water we use so casually on a daily basis.

Jennifer and Anne grew up in drought years in California and are both still very conscious of how precarious our water supply is. An old water-saving trick from back in the day was to fill a quart-size plastic bottle with water (yes, with water) and put it in the back of your toilet tank. The size of the bottle displaces some of the water and gives you an instant somewhat lower-water flushing toilet. There are great low-flush toilets on the market now, but we know that probably isn't what you want to spend your money on at this time of year. Put it on your to-do list for next year.

And here's another idea, and an especially good one for the winter months. Anne's bathwater takes quite a while to heat. While the water is warming, she fills the dog's bowl and also a few other containers with water that she then uses to water plants. And her Christmas resolution is to use the gray water from her bathtub to help flush her toilet.

The Gift of a Smile

Don't be discouraged by all this talk of energy consumption. There are lots of gifts you can give to those around you that don't consume resources—the gift of a smile, a massage, a joke, a song, a poem. These simple gifts don't consume anything, and they actually contribute to the joy and positive energy in the world. Start giving them freely!

Go Organic!

When thinking about our environment there is another big topic—farming. Much of what we eat here in America comes from large corporate farm operations that use pesticides and chemicals, might be experimenting with genetic engineering, and truck their products miles to reach your local store. The Organic Trade Association mounted a successful marketing campaign around Earth Day called "GoOrganic! for Earth Day." For just that one day of the year, eat organic. Christmas could also be another "GoOrganic! Day." This is a wonderful time to focus on where your food comes from and how it is grown. You may well emerge from the holiday season with distinctly different shopping and eating habits.

Organic? How Can I Be So Sure?

"Natural." "Pure." "Safe." A lot of these terms seem to be tossed around without any real meaning. One piece of info you can rely on is the USDA Organic seal, which went into use in 2002. The regulations behind the seal:

● Prohibit the use of irradiation, sewage sludge, or genetically modified organisms in organic production
● Reflect recommendations concerning items on the national list of allowed synthetic and prohibited natural substances

- Prohibit antibiotics in organic meat and poultry
- Require 100 percent organic feed for organic livestock

FOR YOUR GARDEN

Starbucks' Grounds for Your Garden program lets you pick up used coffee grounds that you can spread on your acid-loving plants. A nice holiday gesture would be to get enough to spread around your neighborhood, offering to take care of a few plants for an elderly neighbor or someone who can't work in their own garden.

There are four types of approved labels based on the percentage of organic content. Check the produce or product in question to see if it has any of these:

1. 100 Percent Organic—may carry USDA Organic seal
2. Organic—at least 95 percent of content is organic by weight (excluding water and salt) and may carry the USDA Organic seal
3. Made with Organic—at least 70 percent of content is organic and the front product panel may display the phrase "Made with Organic" followed by up to three specific ingredients (may *not* display the USDA Organic seal)
4. Less than 70 percent of content is organic and may list only those ingredients that are organic on the ingredient panel with no mention of organic on the main panel (may *not* display the USDA Organic seal)

According to the U.S. Department of Agriculture, there are 4.1 million acres of organic farmland now, triple the amount from ten years ago. But a farmer's fields don't turn organic overnight. In fact, it takes three long years before farm fields and whatever grows in them can be certified organic. So what do farmers do in the meantime? They produce something called "transitional." Wal-Mart recently made a big pro-green statement by buying millions of tons of transitional cotton to be used in a line of T-shirts. Why is this pro-green? Because it helps the farmers who are in the middle of making the change and will encourage more growers to go green.

Start Where You Can

Overwhelmed by all these environmental facts and figures? Please don't be. We aren't asking you to reduce your footprint to zero overnight this Christmas, but you might be able to cut it down by 15 percent. If thousands and thousands of us were able to reduce our impact on the environment at Christmas by just 15 percent, it would add up to large numbers. When Jennifer redid the numbers on her Volvo, entering 200 fewer miles driven per year, it dropped from a yearly output of 9,312 pounds of CO_2 to 7,759. So if she just cuts down her driving by that relatively small amount, instant smaller carbon footprint!

Now you have a sampler of the major environmental issues of Christmas—and some ideas on what you can do about them. Christmas has been celebrated since about 350 C.E. Solstice celebrations of the year's shortest day and longest night are even older. For all those years, people have been stopping by each other's homes, swapping gifts, and eating. It's a noble tradition, but as you can see, now our Christmas celebrations put a weight on the world. It's time to put a change to that, so from here on you'll learn more about specific holiday activities, their environmental consequences, and how to best go after the greenest possible Christmas.

Five Green Holiday Environment Ideas

1. Household waste increases 25 percent during the holidays; vow to reduce that number in your life.
2. Remember to recycle all that wrapping paper and all those cards. Seek out goods made from recycled paper or reuse it yourself rather than tossing.
3. Start a Green Logbook and track your habits. List what you consume and what you throw out each day.
4. Green a few holiday traditions by burning fire logs made from recycled material, using LED Christmas lights, and shoveling your driveway instead of using a snow blower.
5. Give a gift to the Earth by giving up bottled water.

3. Money Is Always Green

According to Christian tradition, three Zoroastrian priests, known variously as the Three Wise Men, the Three Kings, or the Magi, followed the Star of Bethlehem, found Jesus, and presented gifts of frankincense, myrrh, and gold. That's where it all got started. The idea of Christmas giving and spending has evolved through the ages. In the Middle Ages, gifts were exchanged between people with a business or legal relationship, like a tenant to a landlord.

Over the years, Christmas evolved into a time for celebration, some of it to excess, while the gift-giving traditions waned. In post–Revolutionary America, the idea of Christmas—considered more of an English custom—fell out of favor altogether. Ironically, Charles Dickens's 1843 novel, *A Christmas Carol*, served to return Christmas to the forefront as a time to reconsider values, including compassion and family goodwill.

Lurking in the background was the idea of Santa Claus, which, prior to the 1920s or so, was embodied in a figure known as Father Christmas. Father Christmas was more associated with merrymaking and drunkenness than gift giving and went by the name of St. Nicholas and other names in other cultures.

To make a long story short, a German-American cartoonist named Thomas Nast developed the modern-day images of Santa Claus in the 1860s, and those images were adopted by American stores and advertisers in the 1920s. From that point forward, the gift-giving traditions went to excess. As they say, the rest is history.

Christmas Spending and Consumption

The plain and simple fact is that we spend a ton of money on Christmas. That's not all bad, for, among other things, it helps the American economy. But too much is too much! Christmas is a great opportunity to take a look at our values and the impact of Christmas spending, not only on the environment but on our own personal finances.

Years of experience gave us the impression that going green is more expensive. Buying organic this, recycled that, or specially prepared something else at a boutique shop or someplace on the Internet adds up. Yet the truth is that going green actually saves money,

CHERRIES GARCIA, PLEASE

Who said environmentalists don't know how to have fun? Mark your calendar for the annual Free Cone Day from Ben & Jerry's in April. Find out this year's date at the Web site *www.benjerry.com*. Be sure to visit their *www.lickglobalwarming.org* site, which has great info on how to put yourself on a carbon emissions diet.

especially at Christmastime. Why? It's all about consumption. We *consume* less. Consuming less costs less. That's a fairly obvious part of the equation. Here's the more subtle part. We're rapidly approaching what author Malcolm Gladwell calls a "tipping point," a point in time, triggered by small events, where what was once universally true is true no longer. The tipping point is caused by the relentless rise in energy costs and the cost of other commodities and resources. The tipping point is this: if it isn't cheaper already, it will just plain cost less to do things the green way, no matter how much we do or consume.

In this chapter we'll show how consuming less and consuming green saves money and how it can help the American economy at the same time. You'll learn to add green "values" to your other Christmas values, and, more than likely, by the end of the chapter you'll vow to spend less on useless things for yourself and others.

The High Cost of Christmas

All day long we make decisions with consequences. We carry a refillable bottle instead of buying a plastic water bottle, and we keep a few ounces of plastic from living in a landfill for a few thousand years. We decide to walk to the post office instead of drive, and we save gas, carbon emissions, and get a little exercise. We shop at the corner store instead of at the megamall, and an independent store lives to see another day.

Looked at this way, your decisions and actions are powerful. Every decision you make supports something. Spending your money and time thoughtfully is a way you can support efforts and trends that you want to see more of and discourage ones you think are harmful. Your dollars, hours, and efforts are powerful social tools!

This is especially true at Christmas. We all spend more between Thanksgiving and New Year's than at any time of the year. Want some figures? According to a Gallup poll done in October 2007, the average American shopper spends $909 on Christmas. In fact, some 35 percent of those polled said they plan to spend more than $1,000, 25 percent between $500 and $1,000, and 30 percent under $500. The rest didn't respond because they didn't know or don't observe the holiday.

That's a heck of a lot of money, and that's *per person*, not per household or per extended family. Given that Americans produce about $45,000 a year in income on average, $909 after-tax dollars is a lot!

Put another way—Americans spent about $161 *billion* on Christmas in 2006. Looking at that figure from the other side of the store counter, Christmas accounted for 25 to 40 percent of all annual income for stores in the United States. So it's a big deal. A big deal in the context of what you spend in a year, and a big deal for the American economy.

It's the Debt, Not Just the Cost

Sad but true, when most Americans spend, they borrow to do it. The Federal Reserve estimates the average household carries $8,500 in credit card debt and that the total consumer debt has grown to some $2.5 *trillion* from $1.7 trillion in 2001 and $355 billion in 1980.

That's huge, but the important part lies in what Christmas and Christmas-related spending can do to your personal debt picture. It's often called the "holiday hangover." Just when other winter-related costs are escalating, like home heating bills, taxes, and so forth, along comes a bulge on those credit cards.

According to another survey, some 30 percent of Americans will pay off Christmas bills within three months of the holiday period, but another 25 percent will carry that debt for more than a year! Now that, on top of what we're spending in the first place, can get pretty expensive. On that $909 we plan to spend apiece

for Christmas, at an 18.9 percent credit card interest rate, it will cost $43 in interest if paid off in three months and $172 if it lingers through the year.

Christmas and Spending—an Extension of Our Values?

Holidays, for most of us, represent time with family, time away from work, and time to recharge and think about what's really important. There's no better time than the holidays to reconnect with our true inner values and what really makes us tick.

That's especially true for people who profess a faith. How we spend our time and money is one of the ways we can live out that faith . . . or deny it. There's an old saying, "Show me your calendar and your checkbook, and I'll show you your values." Christmas is the ultimate example of how this saying plays out in real life.

Christmas can be an opportunity to reassess spending and giving altogether or to realign spending toward products and services consistent with your values. For example, Anne almost never gets around to her Christmas shopping before December 23. Because she lives without a car, it's not easy for her to head to the mall. Instead, she walks to the shopping street a block away and buys everything there. What she buys supports her neighborhood store owners, not some distant corporation she never met. Doing everything on foot keeps a little more carbon dioxide out of the atmosphere.

Can every moment of your Christmas be so deliberate and intentional? No, but overall, the holidays are a wonderful opportunity to live out your values. And if going green is emerging as a priority for you, it's a great time to start. It's a great time to ignore the barrage of commercials headed your way and spend your money consciously and consistently on values and causes and a lifestyle you care about. You'll feel better about yourself, and you'll save money too!

Celebrate Globally, Spend Locally

We just showed how important Christmas is to the American economy. It's important to the local economy too. If spending on Christmas and Christmas gifts is still part of your value system, by all means do it, but, more and more, spending locally is the "green" way to do it.

Spending locally supports local economies. That in turn creates less sprawl and congestion and reduces the amount of physical movement of goods you buy. Supporting local economies, of course, is good for other reasons too. For your own pocketbook, over time, the less physical motion necessary to get a product under someone's Christmas tree, the more you save, especially with today's escalating energy prices. Like many things

green, it's win-win-win—the environment wins, the local economy wins, and your finances win.

The "spend locally" proviso actually occurs on two levels. One, it's good to support your local businesses. Two, for a number of reasons, it's becoming more prudent and more green to buy American where possible and to avoid an overreliance on things made in China—we'll get to the reasons why in a minute.

Support Your Local Business

In Andersonville, Anne's Northside Chicago neighborhood, the concept of local shopping gets a push from a group called Local First Chicago (*www.LocalFirst Chicago.org*). This network of locally-owned independent businesses and friends joined together to keep money and character in Chicago neighborhoods by supporting local businesses. Its Local First campaign is part of a nationwide campaign to educate consumers about the importance of their shopping choices. Recently, Local First Chicago identified ten reasons why shopping in your own back yard is a good idea.

1. *Keep money in the neighborhood.* Studies show that Chicago-owned businesses circulate 70 percent more money back into the local community per square foot than chain stores.

2. *Embrace what makes us different.* Chicago is a city of neighborhoods with local character that chain stores can't capture. "If we wanted to live someplace that looked like everywhere else, we wouldn't be living in Chicago," the group says.

3. *Get better service.* Simple—you know the person behind the counter, and they know you.

4. *Create and keep good jobs.* Nationally, local businesses are the largest employers and account for the majority of job growth. Locally-owned businesses are less likely to pull up stakes and move operations to another city or country, taking jobs with them.

5. *Promote competition and diversity.* A multitude of small businesses, each selecting products based on the needs of their local customers rather than some national sales plan, guarantees a much broader range of product choices.

6. *Less sprawl and environmental damage.* Locally owned businesses can make more local purchases, requiring less transportation, and they generally set up shop in commercial corridors rather than developing out on the fringe.

7. *Support community organizations.* Nonprofits receive an average of 350 percent more support from local business groups than they do from non-locally owned businesses.

8. *Put your taxes to good use.* Local businesses in neighborhoods need comparatively less infrastructure investment and make more efficient use of public services as compared to nationally owned stores entering the community.

9. *Small changes mean large impact.* An Austin, Texas, study showed that if each household redirected just $100 of planned holiday spending from chain stores to locally owned merchants it would create some $10 million in local economic impact.

10. *Invest in the community.* Local businesses are owned by people who live in your neighborhood, work in your neighborhood, and are invested in your community with more than just their dollars.

For these ten reasons and others, Anne's friends and relatives receive microbrewed beer, Swedish coffee bread, imported olive oil, and gift certificates for books—all purchased from the small stores along the store-lined artery Clark Street.

So here's the thing to think about: What specialty stores can you find in *your* neighborhood? What local retailers and craftspeople can you support this holiday while achieving your gift-giving objectives? And how much will you save—and put back into your local economy—by doing so?

Unfair Trade?

"Made in China." It's hard to avoid these days. If you buy a manufactured consumer good—electronics, clothing, toys, home décor, even Christmas cards—it probably says "Made in China" on the box or on the product itself. In fact, according to import-export portal TradeKey (*www.tradekey.com*), there are some 3 million registered importers of Chinese-made Christmas gifts!

In 2007, according to U.S. Census foreign trade figures, we exported $65 billion in goods and services to China while importing some $321 billion for a deficit of some $256.3 billion. That's a lot. And monthly figures rise a lot each year between September and November—because of Christmas.

As unequal as the trade may be between China and the United States, the environmental concerns may be more important. How does China produce goods so cheaply? In part by turning a more or less blind eye to the environment. According to the Council on Foreign

Relations (CFR), China consumed some 2.4 billion tons of coal in 2006—more than the United States, Japan, and the United Kingdom combined. CFR cites Chinese inefficiency from one official: "To produce goods worth $10,000 we need seven times the resources used by Japan, almost six times the resources used by the U.S. and—a particular source of embarrassment—almost three times the resources used by India." And from the vice minister of China's State Environmental Protection Administration (SEPA), in 2005, "The [economic] miracle will end soon because the environment can no longer keep pace."

And that's not all. There are the well-publicized issues of safety, such as the use of lead paint and lead in toys and products for children. That's a green issue too.

As an American individual there isn't much you can do directly to "green" China, but in the context of cutting consumption and helping the U.S. economy, you can make a pact with yourself and your family to buy gifts that are made elsewhere. Do a search on "made in USA" and you'll find lots of suppliers of made in USA products, such as the Web site Still Made in USA (*http://stillmadeinusa.com*). You can really hit your target—especially for toy and child gift buying—at *www.chinafreechristmas.info*.

Green Ideas That Save Green Stuff

The rest of this chapter gives you a sampler of good ideas for the holidays. Most of these topics are covered in more depth in the chapters that follow. Even if you don't use these ideas, we guarantee they'll get you into the green thinking mode. You'll come up with lots of great ideas on your own! And that's really what a green Christmas is all about.

Think Before You Spend

Anne is a longtime frugal person who spends about $350 a year on Christmas, counting presents, entertaining, cards, and decorations. (That, already in and of itself, is a good lesson—how many of you know how much you spend? Count it up. It's a good way to spend a cold, wet Saturday sometime.) Anyway, to people who see excess spending as a patriotic duty or the only proper way to show love and affection, she might seem—well—a little stingy.

Focus too much on the Scrooge side of Anne or anyone else, and you'll miss most of the point: frugality and thrift call for creativity and wit. Not only can it reward your bank account or credit card balance to find a cheaper way—it's a challenge. Really, it's kind of fun. Figuring out how to do something less expensively—getting a lightly used printer from Craigslist instead of buying one

new, or recycling a Christmas tree (see Chapter 5)—feels great. You can share stories about how you saved and how you created value through your own ingenuity.

There's a little thrill about substituting careful thinking for unconscious spending. We don't mean lining up at the mall for deep discounts at dawn the day after Thanksgiving (although that *does* help the bank account!). We mean thinking about purchases ahead of time and looking for significant alternatives to purchasing them in the first place. If you decide to buy anyway, that's okay—just do it deliberately. It's impulse spending that really racks up the debt!

With these ideas in mind, the savings ideas start to gush forth.

- Skip buying wrapping paper this Christmas and wrap your gifts with things you have around the house: newsprint, old paper bags you cover with rubber-stamped designs or old stickers, scraps of fabric, or old gift bags and wrapping you've saved from previous years.
- Skip hosting a big party on your own and find ways to cohost with neighbors.
- Skip buying new clothes for people who might not share your taste anyway and give gift certificates for the best resale shop in your community.

- Skip renting a car on your family vacation and figure out how to get yourselves to airports and back on public transportation.

Most of these ideas are covered later in this book. They're included here just to start you down the track toward savings.

Spend on People and Experiences, Not Things

Buying new "stuff" at the mall may be quick and easy, but in the long run it's not what will make you and your loved ones happy. Just how long will your nephews really play with those marshmallow guns? How many times will Aunt Irma really use that paisley scarf?

Psychologist Daniel Gilbert, director of a laboratory studying the nature of human happiness, has discovered that the best predictor of human happiness is the human relationship. Put simply: the more time we spend with family and friends, the happier we are.

His research has also confirmed that experiences tend to make us happier than stuff. That's because experiences tend to be shared with other people, while objects usually aren't.

So this year try it out for size—spend your Christmas budget on experiences that nurture your relationships with the people around you. Here are more "skips":

- Skip the present and invite a friend over for coffee and conversation by the fire.
- Skip the present and have your kids spend time with grandma and grandpa—maybe playing with the vintage Legos, TinkerToys, and model train equipment that you and your siblings used to enjoy.
- Skip the present and line up a hike in the woods or a meal together. Just hanging out doesn't stress the earth, and will contribute to everyone's happiness.

Keep thinking about what experiences you can "wrap up" for your loved ones.

Spend on Experiences That Build Community

You can spend your money at drive-throughs and on the Internet in lonely splendor, or you can channel it into opportunities to build community. In snowy northern states, winter can be tough on the community spirit. The neighbors you engaged in summertime back-fence chatter are indoors now with the storm windows shut. Chances are good you'll only run into them when there's snow to shovel. Why not invite friends and neighbors to collaborate on an open house, potluck, or progressive dinner that brings them together and lowers the cost and effort for everyone?

During her church's preholiday progressive dinner, Anne always takes the cocktail part, largely because she hasn't got enough chairs for everyone. She serves wine in glasses (not plastic), co-creates a simple menu of appetizers with a friend, turns up the stereo, lights the candles, and opens the door to a few dozen people.

After an hour of socializing—only one hour!—guests help Anne carry the plates and glasses into the kitchen, and everyone, including Anne, goes off on foot to the church just three blocks away. The main course is dished up in the church basement, which has more tables and chairs than a private home.

When that course is over and cleaned up, the group strolls to another home for desserts and champagne—another course that doesn't require a chair for each attendee.

At the end of the evening, everyone is sated and happy—not burned out and broke. Everybody's small contributions add up to one great big holiday party that doesn't burden one host or hostess. And of course, it isn't just church-related events that offer this opportunity. How about your work, or the assisted-living facility your parents or grandparents might reside in? The list is endless. Ask yourself how you can redirect your Christmas budget toward events that bring people together and share expenses.

Reuse Stuff

Not surprisingly, one of the best ways to go green and save money is to use what you already have. Of course, it takes some creativity, but chances are there are a great many things in your house that can be put to use in new ways this holiday season. Remember that 25 percent extra garbage and waste we all produce during the holiday season? By using what you have you can both reduce and reverse that number! And you won't have to go out and buy anything! Here are some ideas for using what you already have to gift wrap:

- *Fabric scraps*—the Japanese have a wrapping art called *furoshiki*, which involves wrapping gifts with cloth. You can give it a try with fabric scraps or perhaps a tea towel or an old scarf you no longer use. Of course there's a Web site—*www.furoshiki .com*!
- *Magazines and newspapers*—brightly colored magazine pages or retro-looking black and white newspaper both make fine wrapping paper and cut down on what gets tossed after using it. Or, for a fine gift, Jennifer likes to buy an inexpensive wood or plastic serving tray, glue on a collage of ads cut from *Vanity Fair* or *W* magazine, and put a clear coat on it.

- *Maps and brochures*—wrap a gift, especially a travel-related gift, with old outdated maps or travel brochures that have been gathering dust on a shelf.
- *Unsalted peanuts*—bet you never thought of using these as packing material instead of those messy foam peanuts. Real unsalted peanuts in the shell work great as packing material, and it's a nice "extra" treat for whoever gets the package.

Buy Used or Recycled Stuff

Recycle and reuse are two major parts of a greener lifestyle. So why not buy used or recycled items? We're not necessarily talking someone else's discards at the local thrift shop—although we're continually surprised at the good stuff one can find. We're talking about vintage or designer products, like clothing, bought from stores specializing in just that. At a thrift store in tony South Lake Tahoe, Jennifer found a flowery Saks Fifth Avenue silk summer dress for a whopping sum of $4. And to dress Peter up for (and after) the holidays, she bought him a barely used Harris Tweed sport coat for $20. Nice.

Think your friends and family will call you cheap? We doubt it. In fact, this can be a creative act that lets you think about finding the perfect gift. A vintage beaded cashmere sweater for your best friend found at a thrift store is much cooler than picking something up at the mall.

Jennifer makes it a point to search out thrift stores and consignment shops in upscale parts of town. You can also check out Vintageous at *www .vintageous.com*. She has found deals on designers like Chanel and Prada, and she finds china and silver to mix and match for friends. Jennifer calls it "OPS"— other people's stuff. She has found amazing things at thrift stores, consignment stores, and garage sales. She figures that what she buys has contributed to the economy twice—once when someone else bought it new and a second time when she bought it used.

Buy Handmade

We've talked about the benefits of buying local. If you buy something local and made by a local craftsperson, you not only support something local in a big way, but you also get something unique, hardly available at the local mall. Why not make this a handmade holiday season? And if you make it yourself, even better.

One sure way to make the holidays better for both yourself and someone else is to buy local art. Of course, you could buy art from a gallery, but that's usually a pretty expensive proposition. Buying from local or neighborhood artists is a better idea, especially if you buy in the neighborhood where your giftee lives.

Local art shows appear in local papers and Web sites, and, of course, you can find people through a network of friends or even local galleries. Anne and Jennifer's brother Paul teaches art to disabled students, and they have a show a few times a year. These are inexpensive but memorable gifts crafted with love and talent by people with few opportunities for self-expression.

If you travel a lot you'll have plenty of opportunities. When Anne travels abroad, she brings back local products like olive oil from Palestine, coffee from Africa, or straw ornaments from Mexico. Buying from street vendors, of course, supports the local economy and often means you're buying directly from the maker.

Share and Share Alike

We're all taught to share from an early age, but as adults, how many of us actually do it to go green or save money? Here's an idea: pool your resources to buy something larger for your extended family that you can all use and share. It can be like forming your own buying club. You can get something bigger and better, such as a family gym membership or a group seating plan for local sports or arts events, with your combined buying power. Of course it takes some cooperation and team-work. But that can be a good thing for the family as well as the finances, right?

And here's a simple green gift idea—offer to share a magazine subscription with a friend or neighbor. Most of us simply cast a magazine into the trash after a few minutes of reading. Why not pass it around to your neighbors? Highlight interesting stories for each other. Heck, if doctors' offices can keep the same magazines for years, two neighbors should be able to share it for a few days, and you'll save subscription costs and countless pounds of unnecessary paper waste. For double green credit, you could subscribe to *Mother Earth News*, and old standbys like *National Geographic* fit well too.

A Word About Ordering Online

Ask yourself which is the greener approach—ordering from catalogs or online and having it shipped to your house, or driving out into your own local neighborhood to buy things? It's a tricky question.

From a money and budget standpoint, it is easier to stay on budget if you go the catalog and online route. You can plan and do research, making calculated lists of what you are buying for whom, and just get it done. If you are out in a bricks-and-mortar store, it is too easy to get dazzled by your environment and get carried away by impulse buys. And you'll spend a lot on gas, lunches, and extra stuff for yourself along the way. Right?

But is it greener to have all of your purchases shipped from one or many warehouses via FedEx or UPS directly to your door? It may depend on where you live and how you do it. If you buy everything at once, the delivery truck can bring most of it at once. Most of us live on a delivery route already, so the driver isn't really making the "special trip" it seems like he or she is making. Some suppliers use U.S. Mail or package delivery services that run local delivery through the U.S. Mail, and that delivery person comes to your house anyway. Ask about DHL's "DHL@home" combined delivery service.

Back to Basics

Of course, not everything about Christmas is about gift buying. Peter loves to calculate how much electricity any given household appliance takes to accomplish its task. For example, microwaving a potato at 600 watts for 6 minutes at the national average of 10.4 cents per kWh comes out to 0.6 kilowatts delivered for one-tenth of an hour at 10.4 cents per hour, or $0.6 \times .1 \times 10.4$, which equals 0.624 cents, or less than a penny. Baking a potato in an oven for 60 minutes at maybe 2,500 watts works out to about 26 cents. Not much difference, but such decisions add up quickly.

Peter also splits his own fireplace kindling from scrap dimensional lumber from discard piles on construction sites (ask before taking, of course!). Peter doesn't *really* spend all his time counting kilowatt-hours, but he knows how to when he needs to.

Jennifer likes to be self-reliant in a sort of upscale pioneer woman way, along the lines of, "I can make my own bread, forage for wild mushrooms, use them to whip up a tasty appetizer, and invite friends over for cocktails." Think Martha Stewart meets the Outdoor Channel. She seldom runs out to the store for "things," preferring to look around and see how she can put something she already has to another use.

Five Green Money Ideas

1. Christmas is a great time to look at the impact your spending has on the environment, and on your personal financial situation.
2. There are many creative ways to show your love without buying a gift.
3. Buy local to help small merchants, drive less, and support your neighborhood economy.
4. Catalog shopping keeps you off the road and cuts down on impulse buying at the mall.
5. Buy used or recycled products as unique gifts that keep valuable goods in circulation and out of landfills.

4. Eco-Family Time

Winter can be a wonderful time to focus on the natural world around us. Christmas itself can be a wonderful time to help your children open their eyes to what is already there and the critical role they can help play in preserving it. Just as your favorite holiday memories probably revolve around quiet moments, so too do the best moments you spend with your kids, such as a walk in the woods, a day at a lake, or a morning at the zoo. Take the time this holiday to plan low-key family time that doesn't involve lots of money, lots of travel, or lots of stress.

Get started early in the month with the simple act of choosing a tree. In Chapter 5, you'll learn much more than you care to about the real versus fake tree debate, but why not include your children in the discussion? Let them help you decide which way to go. If you go for a live tree, let them help choose which tree farm you visit. Going to a local tree farm is a good time to talk to your kids about the reasons we need small farms and the reasons that acres and acres of living trees are good for the environment. A day in the woods with children, trees, and the promised cup of hot chocolate makes for a splendid holiday memory.

After the holidays are over, you can involve the children in what happens to the tree. Taking it to the composting station? Let them help you drag it to the car. Find a tree dropoff in your area at *www.Earth911.com*. You might also ask your children for creative ideas on what to do with the tree instead of composting. "Can we make it into paper?" wondered eight-year-old Jonathan Sander about the family tree last year.

Play in the Kitchen

In the book *Animal, Vegetable, Miracle*, writer Barbara Kingsolver described her family's attempt to only eat food that was grown in their neighborhood or that they grew themselves. If it didn't meet either of those criteria, they'd learn to do without.

So what about the holidays smack dab in the middle of winter? Kingsolver writes, "We are a household of mixed spiritual backgrounds, and some of the major holidays are not ours, including any that commands its faithful to buy stuff nobody needs. But we celebrate plenty. We give away our salsas and chutneys as gifts, and make special meals for family and friends: turkey and stuffing." Kingsolver and her husband, along with their two daughters, learned to do it together. The girls raised chickens (and sold eggs to their mother!), grew bean sprouts in glass jars, and helped with the canning. When the year was over, they knew how long it took to raise food, what was in season and when, and just how their food got to the table.

Is there a simple kitchen skill that you could teach your children this year as a new family tradition? Jennifer taught her boys how to make a simple bread recipe from a book called *Artisan Bread in Five Minutes*. The recipe really does only take five minutes, and now both boys can make their own bread. They also have a heightened sense of what good bread tastes like—no more squishy white bread for them!—and will forever seek out homemade artisan bread rather than bite into some factory-produced loaf. Plan an afternoon or two around the kitchen table making cookies, bread, muffins, or homemade play dough! The recipe is simple:

Homemade Play Dough

2 cups flour
1 cup salt
2 cups water
2 tablespoons vegetable oil
3 teaspoons cream of tartar

Directions: Mix all ingredients in a saucepan over low heat until the dough will roll into a ball. Store in an airtight container.

Cut-Up Crafts

Haul out all those old Christmas cards you've been saving for years, sit your children down on the floor with scissors they can use, and have them help you make small greeting cards, place cards, thank-you notes, gift tags, or paper ornaments with the old cards. All you need are a stack of cards, scissors, tape or glue, and some imagination! You can also cut the cards up and use the pieces to piece together your own paper village of gingerbread houses.

HOLIDAY TREASURES

Christmas morning can be even more exciting for the children if you hide their presents around the house and give them each a treasure map to follow. You won't have to wrap the presents and can skip creating paper waste. It adds to the wonder and newness of the day and prolongs the experience for both children and parents.

Quiet Time

Why not take this opportunity to sit down together every night in the few days before Christmas and read stories out loud? It's a wonderful time to read Dickens's *A Christmas Carol*. Young children will love the spookiness of it and all that talk of the "ghost of Christmas Present." Try to read by the light of just your Christmas tree and a glowing fire.

Does your local library rent DVDs? Skip the crowds and the cost down at Blockbuster and see if your local public library branch has any family holiday films you can all watch together. You've seen *It's a Wonderful Life* a zillion times, but your kids probably haven't. The live-action Jim Carrey version of *The Grinch Who Stole Christmas* does a nice job of reminding us all that "Christmas doesn't come in a box . . ."

An evening spent sharing stories or DVDs can include the special treat of sleeping near the Christmas tree. Bring out the sleeping bags and let them snuggle up. Not too close to the tree and the lights, and please remember to turn the lights off. Don't leave them on all night while the children are sleeping nearby.

Seven Great Green Ways to Spend Family Time Together

Spend money? Buy things? Drive somewhere? Who needs it when you can:

1. *Play sudoku together*. This numbers game will absorb anyone who sits down to try. Sudoko puzzles are printed in many newspapers, and there is an online site devoted to it: *www.websudoku.com*.

Available for all ages, these puzzles will keep you all going mentally.

2. *Play Hangman.* What do you need other than a scrap of paper, a pencil, and your own imagination? Hangman is a wonderful way for kids and grownups to interact and can keep you all laughing for hours.

3. *Invent your own knock-knock jokes.* Go ahead, make up some corny jokes! Start with the punch line or a funny word or saying, and then work backwards.

4. *Bring out the board games.* Drag out those board games and get down on the floor! It is a great low-cost way to spend a green afternoon, nothing to buy, nothing to consume. Chances are you have several old family favorites that your kids would love to play again.

5. *Create your own arts and crafts.* Use the materials you have on hand; old paper grocery bags make art paper. You can use it to make paper gingerbread men by tracing cookie cutters on the spread-out bag, cutting them out, and decorating with crayons, scraps of paper or material, or old buttons.

6. *Share family stories.* The holidays are a wonderful time to tell your children about your own childhood or your family history. Gather in front of the tree, turn out the room lights and turn on the tree lights, and sit together in the glow with mugs of hot chocolate.

You could also make a video together to e-mail to friends and relatives and skip sending cards all together this year.

7. *Take a nature walk.* Peter and Jennifer established a simple New Year's tradition when their children were small. On New Year's Day the family goes to a nature preserve to see the thousands of snow geese that winter there. Pack a lunch, tie up your hiking boots, and wander around trying to see how many different kinds of birds are there. The amazing sound of honking geese and the crisp holiday season air is not to be missed.

Reduce Your Family's Footprint

Make it a family contest to see who can get through the day producing the least amount of waste, using the least energy, or consuming the fewest resources. Children will love the chance to catch you consuming too much and will soon be scolding you about leaving the coffee pot plugged in, tossing out paper rather than putting it in the recycling bin, or walking out of the room without flicking off the lights. Make scorecards and post them prominently; let the children keep score, and they will get into the game right away. Pay them a quarter every time they catch you doing something ungreen. Don't forget to award prizes.

The Christmas Bird Count

For more than one hundred years the National Audubon Society has been holding an annual Christmas Bird Count around the country, relying on amateur birders to help keep track of the health of the bird population. Anyone can participate, and you can find the details for this year's bird count at *www.audubon.org/bird/cbc*.

The next bird count takes place between December 14, 2008, and January 5, 2009. Choose a day in that time period, set aside an hour to conduct your count, and start birdwatching! It only takes an hour, so even small children can participate without losing interest. Don't worry, you won't have to endlessly scan the horizon with binoculars. The process is simple—all you need to do is draw an imaginary circle in the area you want to watch and keep track of how many birds enter into your circle area. Your imaginary circle could be in the back yard or front yard, on the deck, or in whatever area you choose.

Another yearlong bird counting project is conducted through Project FeederWatch. You watch the birds at the feeder and report in every so often. The information at the site *www.feederwatch.org* contains ways you can use this as a science or math project for kids.

Spending Christmas Day focused on wildlife is a great way to remember that our planet depends on us to take care of it. One eco-friendly mom recommends taking your Christmas tree outside when you are done with it after the big event and turning it into a bird feeder for the rest of the winter. Prop it up in a planter and hang birdseed balls that will help keep your local songbirds fed during the slim winter months.

Pray for Snow

Outdoor sports and activities help kids understand our relationship to the natural world and to changing weather patterns. Having grown up on the slopes, both Anne and Jennifer have made skiing a part of their own children's lives. What better way to make your children aware of global warming than by having them focus on the snow report!

Up in the Sierra Nevada Mountains, Jennifer's kids keep an eye on the snow pack (which they also know is connected to how much water is available later in the spring), and in the Midwest Anne's son Alex keeps an eye on the snow pack at his favorite resort. The skiing cousins are also focused on just when the ski resorts open and close—an early opening means that winter has come early, and a late close—May 4 at one California resort last year—means there was more snow than usual!

Another outdoor winter activity is ice skating, an inherently green event because many people share the equipment by renting it rather than everyone purchasing their own. Snowshoeing takes you through the pristine woods and meadows, no gas, no carbon. Not so great, at least greenwise, are activities like snowmobiling. The gas-powered engines create quite a bit of CO_2 and noise.

Take 'em to the Dump!

Kids love to go to the dump with their parents. What excitement! Huge mounds of trash, trucks and forklifts, seagulls and crows everywhere. It's like being inside a children's picture book—look over there at the big yellow truck, honey! So why not plan a family outing to the dump this year? It is an eye-opener that will leave an impression on every member. Small kids will remember the sheer size of everything, the big piles of garbage. Bigger kids will see how much effort is involved in removing trash once they toss it in a bin. And as for us adults, it is a great visual reminder of the waste process as well as a glimpse at what everyone else tosses out. You'll see more than one perfectly usable item that someone somewhere had grown tired of and pitched rather than find another way to use it or give it to someone who will.

The family that visits the dump happily together will probably recycle happily together too. Green your family by getting the kids involved as early as possible. "My four-year-old takes the cans and bottles out," says Geraldine Fitzgerald Anders, the founder of the cloth napkin company Fabikins. She started her company because she wanted her children to understand that small steps—like using cloth napkins instead of paper—can make a difference. "Children learn by watching their parents' actions, so we all need to make sure we are setting good green examples ourselves."

Green Teens and Their Money

As recommended in Chapter 1, it's critical to get your family to buy in to the idea of having a green Christmas. The more they agree with your vision of how to do things differently this year, the better it will go. Have your teenagers bought in? Sure. They've been listening to the messages about how to save the environment since they started grade school. This will not be new material. In fact, they can probably tell you a fact or two.

American teenagers have awesome buying power, and their dollars can make a difference too. The Web site I Buy Different, at *www.ibuydifferent.org*, is sponsored by both the Center for the New American Dream and the World Wildlife Fund. It has age-appropriate

information on how teens can increase their consumer savvy and see the link between their purchases and the wider world. If just one in every ten middle school or high school students each decided to buy one recycled paper notebook instead of one with nonrecycled paper, it would mean a savings of 60,000 trees, 25.5 million gallons of water, and prevent 5,250,000 pounds of global warming gases from being released. Pretty powerful stuff!

GREEN DOGS AND CATS

Don't forget those other family members—cats and dogs. There are biodegradable kitty litters available (*www.naturesearth.com*), healthy vegetarian pet food (*www.petpromise .com*), and you can find ideas on nontoxic flea control at *www .alt4animals.com*.

Composting for Children

Give your children pets for Christmas. Not the warm, furry ones—instead, lots and lots of wiggly ones! A worm box for kitchen composting is a fun thing to involve the children in. They will learn how worms break down food scraps and can be put in charge of the process of taking care of the box. "When school children visit our worm farm and see what goes on it really gives them a sense of their connection to nature," the folks who run The Worm Farm in Durham, California, tell us. "And you can watch recycling in action with our Worm Vue Wonder!"

This see-through worm viewer is the worm version of an ant farm. The clear plastic box lets you watch what goes on in a worm's day. Available from *www.thewormfarm .net,* you will still need worms to go with it. Find them in your back yard, or order them from The Worm Farm or also Blue Belly Farm at *www.bluebellyfarm .com.* Putting children in charge of an outdoor garden composting project is also ideal. The same kinds of kitchen scraps the worms will eat can be put in a composter, keeping pounds of waste out of the landfill every week and creating loamy compost to use in your garden.

Although getting a box of worms would be a cool gift for a kid, finding a large green plastic composter under the tree on Christmas morning probably wouldn't thrill anyone. Buy one for the family, learn how to use it together, and then the children can take turns going out to the composter with the kitchen scraps you've collected, dumping them in, and periodically turning the composter or stirring it to keep the action going inside.

For a real hands-on family building project you can get plans to build several kinds of composters at *www*

.bluegrassgardens.com, or you can get a basic plastic bin composter at Ace Hardware for about $75.

Plan Your Green Garden Now

Starting your children in the garden is also a good green habit. Work together to find the perfect spot in your yard or patio, then sit down and plan what you are going to plant (make sure to plant everyone's favorite vegetables!) and who is going to be in charge of keeping it neat and tidy.

There are many planning tasks that can keep kids busy over the winter months until the growing season begins. Winter is when you can start collecting seed catalogs. Request free catalogs from *www.burpee.com* or *www.cooksgarden.com* to share with the children.

Sending the kids into the garden to pick fresh corn, spinach, or squash will create memories for a lifetime as well as healthy eating habits. Getting started with small live plants is easier than trying to grow from seed. Mother Earth News sells garden sets, like Heirloom Tomatoes or Rainbow Bell Peppers, at *www.motherearthnews.com/gardensbox* that ship when spring begins.

Down Home(school) Ideas

Our friend Jasmin Mutabdzija homeschools her two young girls and shared these ideas for parents:

"As a homeschooling family, our house is always overflowing with art and craft projects. When Christmastime comes around, we gather the piles of duplicate photos and paintings that have gathered over the year and paste them into scrapbooks. These scrapbooks have become famous over the years. Everyone loves the personalized touch, and it keeps the grandparents who live far away up to date. It also helps alleviate the bulging box in the closet I keep for my own memory books. We also have fun making presents for our homeschooling friends. Brushing up on our fractions, we measure out the recipe ingredients for breads, brownies, and cookies. We then decorate the homemade gift by pasting a little printout of the recipe on a glass jar we have recycled from something else or found at our recycling center.

"For those I know who have dietary restrictions, we usually like to give plants. We plant herb seeds in little biodegradable containers and then give them away when they begin to sprout. These starters are great because they do not take up too much room inside while waiting for spring, and the kids love eating what is growing in their kitchen. We have found that the people around us appreciate the effort and thought that goes in to our gifts. Big plastic toys lose their appeal quickly. Baking and planting are activities that encourage family time, which never goes out of style."

Focusing your family activities around a green theme can be extremely rewarding. Come next Christmas you will have a house full of children who are experts at reducing, reusing, and recycling! Remember, though, that the greenest gift you can give your children is your undivided attention. It doesn't cost anything, it doesn't produce waste, and it doesn't consume resources. Just sit next to them on the couch and a whole afternoon will slip by.

Five Eco-Family Time Ideas
1. Get your children involved early in becoming a greener family.
2. Work together to recycle old holiday cards into new cards, gift tags, and place cards.
3. Gardening and composting are excellent ways to get children thinking about our planet.
4. Set aside time to do nothing with children, just hang out and enjoy.
5. Enjoy the outdoors together whenever you can.

5. Green Holiday Decorating

Part of the magic of Christmas comes from the fact that things *look* different. Our houses, inside and out, don't look the way they do the other eleven months of the year. Our houses look special in a way that reminds us of the reason for the season. Decorations and symbols are visual clues and instant emotional triggers that reach us in a meaningful way, making us smile at an old holiday memory or our hearts beat a tiny bit faster in anticipation of something special happening this year.

Lights and greenery hark back to earlier times when in the dead of winter an evergreen tree could remind us of the eventual return of spring, and flickering candles could help us remember the return of the sun. Bringing evergreen boughs into your house was also an ancient fertility symbol.

You've just read through several chapters with lots of information on waste and consumption. Is that some-

thing you need to keep in mind yet again when thinking about how to decorate in a greener manner? Well, there will be a few things for you to consider here about the impact that your decorating decisions could have.

Let's start with the single biggest form of holiday decoration for most of us . . . the Christmas tree. And what could be greener, right? Maybe. Americans buy close to 30 million real Christmas trees every year. They also buy a substantial number of artificial trees.

Deciding on a Tree

Who knew choosing a tree could be so fraught with concerns. Real or fake—which is the greener choice? It's easy to be dazzled by the magazine ads for the "finest" artificial Christmas trees, which come "pre-lit" with "energy-saving LEDs." Energy-saving? Gee, it must be good and green then, right? Even our own eco-conscious neighbor across the street now questions whether she made the right decision years ago when she bought a large artificial tree. "I thought I was being so green, saving a tree. And now I wonder . . . but at least I'm going to use it forever."

The side-by-side comparison detailed on the following pages outlines some of the environmental issues encountered when choosing between a real or artificial Christmas tree.

REAL TREES	ARTIFICIAL TREES
Place of Origin	
United States and Canada	85 percent from China
Method of Production	
Farming • Planting takes place Jan.–May • Estimated 40–45 million trees planted in 2007 in North America • Estimated 446 million trees growing on farms in U.S. • Free farms support complex ecosystems	Factory • Raw materials sent to factory and assembled into final product • Product is shipped to U.S. then distributed to stores • Number of factories unknown • Factories only consume natural resources
Components	
Plant tissue • 100 percent biodegradable	Plastics and metals • Nonbiodegradable
PVC Free?	
Yes	No
Lead Free?	
Yes	No • Lead is used in the process of making PVC plastic
Carbon Neutral?	
Yes • Trees absorb carbon dioxide • When decomposing, carbon, nitrogen, and other elements are released into soil	No • Plastic is a petroleum byproduct
Disposal	
Recycled • Used trees can be recycled in a variety of ways • Decomposing trees add nutrients back into the earth	Landfill • Fake trees can't be recycled and end up in landfills • All of the accumulated fake trees are a burden to the environment indefinitely

  Green Christmas

REAL TREES	ARTIFICIAL TREES
Chemicals?	
No	Yes
• Scientists have measured cut Christmas trees for chemical reside and not found any significant amounts • Many different bugs, fungi, and parasites can attack and kill trees, so farmers may use pesticides to keep consumers' trees healthy and alive until harvest • Most pesticides are ground applied • Herbicides are used to suppress, not kill off, weeds to prevent soil erosion • If someone tells you there are chemicals on cut Christmas trees, they are wrong	• PVC is a dangerous chemical • Manufacture of PVC creates and disperses dioxins, toxic manmade chemicals • Released into air or water, dioxins enter the food chain where they accumulate in fatty tissues of animals and humans, a potential risk for causing cancer, damaging immune functions, and impairing children's development
Renewable Resource?	
Yes	No
• New trees are planted every year	• Petroleum, used to make plastic, is a non-renewable resource, as are metals
Eco-Friendly	
Yes	No

Full disclosure: This chart came from the National Christmas Tree Association, but the issues are pretty clear here. Is it better to buy one of the live trees that cover some 500,000 acres of land around the country, or something that arrives on a boat from China?

Boto, a Chinese Christmas tree manufacturer owned by the Carlyle Group, is the largest manufacturer of artificial trees. They employ 8,000 workers at a three-million-square-foot factory in Shenen and make 400 different types of trees. Is that a good thing for our environment? Buying a live tree, particularly if it comes from a locally owned tree farm in your area, is the greener way to go.

But then what? You chop down a living tree, have it in your house for just a few weeks, and after the ornaments are packed away, what happens to it? For many years the dump was the destination of most trees, but in the last few decades, mulching trees after the holiday is over has become a national tradition. Treecycling! You can find a mulching operation near you by going to *http://www.earth911.org* and typing in your zipcode.

New York City's Mulchfest 2008 (which ran the first few days of the year) crunched up 13,137 trees, a 14 percent increase from the trees left over after the 2007 holidays. What happens to all of this chopped-up-tree mulch? It gets put to use in many ways, including spreading it on hiking trails and beachfronts to prevent erosion or using it as fish habitat.

Alterna-Trees

Does Christmas always require a noble fir? Maybe not. In San Francisco, the Friends of the Urban Forest (*www.fuf.org*) will drop off a live tree in early December and then pick it up again after the holidays are over. These are not your typical Christmas trees though. These trees will later find homes on the city streets in neighborhoods that need the shade.

"For people who are looking for an alternative to a tree that's been cut, and a tree that will live on and has the added benefit of giving back to your city, this is the tree and the program for them," says Kelly Quirke, the executive director of Friends of the Urban Forest. For around $100, San Francisco folks can call them and have a tree delivered in December and picked up after the holidays are over. Try a Southern magnolia, a strawberry tree, or a New Zealand Christmas tree. All are between seven and twelve feet tall and, as Kelly points out, sturdy enough to hang lights and ornaments on!

MADE IN THE USA

Still thinking about getting an artificial tree you can reuse? How about getting an American-made tree, then. Check out the lead-free offerings at *www.uschristmastree.com*.

The Recycled Christmas Tree

Have you ever thought about using a recycled tree? Anne has had a recycled tree *twice.* The first opportunity turned up at a pre-Christmas party. When she complimented her hostess on the beautiful tree, her hostess friend sighed and said it was too bad the tree was coming down the next day because they were leaving town. In Chicago, taking down your tree means walking it out to the alley. These hosts had a pickup truck. Anne suggested they throw the tree into their truck, drive the truck to her house, and throw the tree into her back yard. They did, and Anne had a beautiful Scotch pine cut by the neighbors from their land in Wisconsin—for free!

The second year's tree was less successful. Again, Anne received a Wisconsin tree from a friend leaving town for the holidays, but this tree was so skimpy and stressed it barely survived the transfer and spent the Christmas holiday shedding sad little needles.

Still, for two years, Anne saved $60 and a tree's life. And if the right tree comes along, she'll try it again. In Chicago, discarded trees turn up in the alley by December 23, and because scavenging from the alley is a time-honored Chicago tradition, she wouldn't feel embarrassed to drag one home. This might be awkward, or even prohibited, in your community, but if you can arrange a hand-me-down from friends and then revive the old tradition of putting up the tree on Christmas Eve, your recycled tree can cap off your green Christmas.

Going Treeless

Now that Anne is an empty nester, a tree is less important to her holiday decorating scheme. Last year, she skipped a tree altogether. Three dollars worth of branches from the Christmas tree lot, a spool of floral

wire, and an evening spent watching a chick flick on her DVD player were all it took for her to make a lovely evergreen swag that she hung up in the archway between her living and dining rooms. From it she hung Swedish straw ornaments and Danish stars, and, presto!, her home looked like an illustration by the Swedish artist Carl Larssen. And since the swag hung from the ceiling and had no lights, it could stay up while she was out of town. Sixty more dollars and one more tree saved!

The two hours she spent on this craft project were no more than she would have spent decorating a full-size tree. Empty nesters like Anne can really be flexible about holiday habits and decorations.

- Hang decorations on the ficus tree in the living room that you already have.
- Anne's friends Sue and Phil still use the artificial tabletop tree that daughter Evelyn begged for when she was eleven years old. That was ten years ago, and while Evelyn has outgrown her dolls, everyone still loves the tree and its exquisite miniature ornaments.
- Skip a tree altogether and instead use an evergreen swag, a fir tree branch in a vase, or a greenery-covered mantelpiece to make your home feel festive. This could be the year you bust out and try to establish a new nontree tradition!

Another fun alternative to traditional trees is citrus trees in boxes, the kind on wheels. Think about how fabulous lemon, lime, or grapefruit trees would look with a strand of LED holiday lights and a light sprinkling of your favorite ornaments!

Unplug the Tree

How about giving this a bit of thought and skipping the lights altogether for a year? Stringing old-fashioned strands of cranberries or popcorn (air-popped organic, please!) will keep the children busy and give your tree a sweetly vintage feel. Or try something less old-fashioned but still effective—Hershey's Kisses. They're a treat to look forward to when the tree comes down.

Decoration Swap

A tree laden with glittery decorations is a grand holiday touch. If you already own lots of decorations, no need to buy more. But if you are tired of the way your old stuff looks, how can you freshen up your decorations without either consuming more or adding to the waste pile? You can invite friends over for a trading night with ornaments. Please don't just toss out the ones you don't use or like anymore. Can you give them to a church or an organization that will use them or pass them to someone who will? We are all trying to reduce waste this holiday. So look at

your old decorations and try to come up with ways to reuse or recycle them.

No Points for Poinsettias

Poinsettias might not be your best choice for an eco-friendly holiday. Yes, we know they are actually red, and they sure are pretty, but if you think about how far most of them are trucked—80 percent come from one single grower in Southern California—they really aren't what you could call green. Poinsettias are (thanks to the marketing by the grower) the very emblem of Christmas but aren't native to our soil. A native of Mexico, they don't last much longer than the holidays.

Short-lived in our own environment, most end up in landfills once the decorations come down. "If you leave them on your porch, they die. If you leave them in your house, they die. So what's the point?" asks master gardener Sheri Fischer of The Flower Farm Nursery in Loomis, California. For a longer-lasting plant with color that pops, she suggests using cylcomen, which have wonderful red blooms and come back every year.

Sheri also recommends checking with your local farm exchange office to find out what kinds of plants are best for your local wildlife. "At Christmas, think of what you can plant to help wildlife, like holly berries for the birds. It is a gift to give to the critters in your area."

When adding holiday flowers to your house, make sure you are buying flowers that are in season rather than flowers that have been flown thousands of miles. Flowers in season in December include:

- Amaryllis
- Daffodil
- Darnellia
- Ginestra
- Hyacinth
- Mimosa
- Paperwhite narcissus
- Star of Bethlehem

Many types of flowers—fressia and gardenias, also eucalyptus leaves and fallen branches—are available year-round though, so you can also add these without fear.

Can you go organic with flowers? Absolutely. Using fewer toxic products (or none at all) when growing anything is better for the environment. Just like with your local food growers, look for local flower growers too. Fully 79 percent of the flowers sold in the United States are grown elsewhere, mostly in warm countries like Colombia or Ecuador. So as with any of your purchases, keep it local when you can. When you can't, check out the flowers and wreaths at *www.organicbouquet.com*.

Gather Your Own
Simple materials to make your own wreaths, swags, and spot decorations include eucalyptus, white pine,

spruce, redwood, noble fir, magnolia, English holly, and bay leaves. Peter and Jennifer are lucky enough to live in a neighborhood with lots of trees and open space in a common area, giving them access to several kinds of winter berry bushes, two or three different types of fir trees, and even wild horse chestnuts. Jennifer goes out in early December with a pair of garden shears and collects enough to decorate the house in an hour or so. She hasn't bought a decoration in several years, preferring her more natural look to anything available in a store.

What if you don't have access to natural materials? Chances are you know someone who does, and if you ask around your circle of friends will uncover the perfect garden. Let everyone know that you plan to decorate your house with natural materials this year and that you would be interested in helping someone pick up fallen branches from pines and firs in their yard or would happily trim back an overgrown holly bush in exchange for taking some of the cuttings home. One thing you *can't* do is walk into a park with your clippers and help yourself to what's there. That's against the law, not to mention not very nice.

Foraging Inside

You can also gather pretty things up on the inside of your house to turn into Christmas decorations. Have fun

No Christmas balloons, please. You probably weren't going to decorate with balloons, but it is worth mentioning in case you were thinking about using them at a New Year's Eve party. There is no such thing as an earth-friendly balloon. Skip them all together.

picking out treasures that you don't look at very often or don't set out all year long. Although Anne made her holiday swag out of a few branches, Jennifer makes one every year from a long narrow piece of old silk she drapes underneath the fireplace mantle and festoons with costume jewelry like rhinestones and ropes of pearls. In a later chapter you will read about the annual pirate dinner she hosts, so her silky flashy swag fits the theme well!

Light Up the Holidays with Organic Candles

Nothing creates atmosphere like a scented candle, and nothing creates a green atmosphere like an organic candle! Why use a soy candle? Innovators in the United States developed soybean wax around 1995 in order to replace paraffin wax (which is refined from crude oil and can emit toluene, benzene, formaldehyde, and soot when burned). They invented a wax made from a renewable soybean oil resource in plentiful supply from the farms of America. It is a wax that does not emit the harmful aromatic hydrocarbons of paraffin and produces very little soot.

What is an organic candle? Sounds weirder than the idea of organic flowers. You'd eat a flower before you eat a candle. Remember the National Organic Program that became the law of the land in October 2002? Agricultural products that use the term "organic" must be produced in accordance with established organic standards. These standards were designed for foods and also cover farm practices for fibers such as cotton and wool and agricultural ingredients in personal care products such as soaps and cosmetics. Organic candles and organic wax are new to the marketplace. Lumia Organics of Boulder, Colorado, was the first company to make wax from organic soy oil and the first to apply for organic certification for wax from vegetable oil.

"Remember when you choose your candles that the use of organic candles supports organic farmers," Richard Roth of Lumia (*www.lumia.us*) points out. "Buying and using organic candles helps further the aims of the international organic movement." What are their most popular items in December? "Cinnamon Spice and Evergreen scented candles, of course!" he said.

Lights, Lights, and More Lights

Establish a new tradition by waiting until Christmas Eve to put up your outdoor lights. You can tell the children that it's to let Santa see the house better. Once Santa has spotted the house and made his drop, go ahead and take them down again a few days later as they have served their purpose. It will give more meaning to the light display, save money on your energy bill, and not use as many resources. Another approach is to decide on a set time for festive hours when you flip the switch on your light display. Perhaps every night from 6 to 8 P.M.? Whatever you decide, try to stick to it rather than have your lights on from whenever you remember to turn them on to whenever you remember to turn them off! The electric bill will certainly stay under better control.

In Chicago, Anne participates in Residential Hourly Energy Pricing (RHEP), a conservation program in which consumers are motivated to cut back on their electricity use by paying the actual cost of energy per hour instead of the averaged price that a utility charges most customers. This is great, but the hours of highest prices tend to coincide with the hours of greatest use, and at Christmas that means all the hours when Christmas lights are on. Switching to LEDs would probably help this, but when she wants to have the outdoor lights on between 6 and 11, peak usage and billing times, she doesn't run the dishwasher, the washing machine, or other appliances to offset some of that usage.

Decorating for the holidays gives you so many opportunities to go green, how are you going to use them all? When decorating this year, try to stick to a natural theme. Chances are if what you are decorating with used to be a part of a plant, it is green. If it grew somewhere near your house, even greener! If you don't have to plug it in, you are moving in the green direction! And if it used to be something else—a clear glass bowl on a table filled with ornaments you don't want to hang anymore, or a long strand of costume jewelry pearls that you use as a garland—that is green too. And if it used to belong to someone else and you traded for some of their old things, or it's something you can reuse—awesome!

Five Green Decorating Tips to Remember

1. Choose a living tree from a tree farm in your area.
2. Consider decorating an indoor plant instead of a tree.
3. Organize an old ornament swap among friends rather than tossing or buying new.
4. Make your own wreaths and swags from what grows in your yard or at a friend's house.
5. Turn outdoor holiday lights on for a set period only each night.

6. Green Christmas Entertaining

Holiday parties are a delight for both guests and hosts, aren't they? Well, mostly. Throwing a party can be stressful at times, and even attending a party can be a bit fraught with anxiety. So let's try to keep it simple here in the green entertaining section, simple in both form and content. No need to call in the caterers—there are some low-key ideas you can do yourself.

One thing we think you should avoid doing is lecturing your guests about their own lives. Keep the focus on having a good time rather than making a big point about how eco-friendly your party is. No waving the recycled paper napkins around like Earth Day flags. Okay, maybe you can casually mention that you made it a point to have a greenish sort of a party, but keep it light.

In an Earth Day article for the *New York Times Magazine*, Michael Pollan, author of *The Omnivore's Dilemma* and *In Defense of Food*, put it this way: ". . .

the climate-change crisis is at its very bottom a crisis of lifestyle—of character,
even. The Big Problem is nothing
more or less than the sum total of
countless little everyday choices,
most of them made by us (consumer spending represents 70
percent of our economy), and
most of the rest of them made in
the name of our needs and desires
and preferences." Why do we quote
him here? Because we want to again
stress that your seemingly mundane decisions, decisions about what to serve your guests or how
to serve your guests, really can have an impact on what
Pollan calls The Big Problem. We hope these ideas for
green holiday parties, eco-friendly entertaining, greening your annual office party, and more will inspire you!

**C'EST LE
CHAMPAGNE**
Green Christmas advice
from a French friend, who firmly
believes we should all "Drink lots of
champagne. In magnums, it's more
economical and less glass is used."
C'est la vie!

Inviting Your Guests

So, you're having a party! Wonderful! The holidays are
truly a party season, but now the green questions set
in. Should you send out paper invitations to your guest
list? What about those e-mail Evite thingies?

If you are having a small get-together for a few
friends, why not sit down and handwrite a few personal

invitations instead of going the preprinted party invite route? Everyone loves a handwritten note, and none of us get enough of them nowadays. Sending a personal note will be a wonderful way to get your guests to begin looking forward to the wonderful evening they will soon be enjoying with you.

- Find beautiful handmade papers to use as notes at *www.handmade-paper.us.* Include a small sprig of greenery to add a holiday touch.
- Use a card that becomes something else. Botanical Paperworks, at *www.botanicalpaperworks.com*, has a wide selection of handmade paper cards that contain seeds embedded in the paper. Send out invitations to a party, and your guests will be able to plant the invitation in their garden!
- If you're having more then fifteen guests for a casual party at home, go ahead and use Evite (*www .evite.com*). Sending one of those establishes in your guests' minds that this will be a fairly casual affair, so don't expect them to arrive in black tie if all you have sent is an e-mail.

Before Your Guests Arrive

So much of hosting a party involves the dull job of cleaning before everyone arrives. This year you can be extra good to your guests and use non-toxic cleaning supplies before the big night. Go green by choosing cleaning products without ingredients like chlorine, phosphates, or fragrances. Baking soda can be used as a natural scouring powder on tiles and sinks—just mix up a paste of water and powder and scrub. You can also use it to eliminate odors before your guests arrive. Sprinkle it on the couch or the carpet, let it sit fifteen minutes, then vacuum it up to remove any unpleasant odors. Jennifer likes to mix up chopped rosemary or lavender from the garden with the baking soda she sprinkles on the floor to add a bit of natural scent (you can set some aside from the summer months too). That way you can skip using those spray-on fragrances or odor removers. Here's another recipe for a green cleaner:

ONE OF TO NONE OF

Do you really need a new party dress? Probably not. Why not ask a friend if you can shop her closet? Or go in together to buy one new outfit that you can both wear to different parties. This will help you cut down on buying one-time-use items.

White Vinegar Cleaner

1 cup white vinegar
1 gallon water

Directions: Mix together and use as a simple cleaning solution. Do not use on acid-sensitive surfaces like marble. This solution both cleans and kills bacteria.

NONTOXIC HOUSEKEEPING

Log on to *www.lowimpactliving.com* to find lists of housekeeping businesses around the country that use nontoxic products.

Anne thinks we shouldn't forget good old Murphy's Oil soap and Bon Ami. These are old green products still on the shelf. Actually, Bon Ami has lost its shelf space in lots of places. Ask for it to try to bring it back! Bon Ami contains no chlorine, dye, or perfume, which means it's less polluting to make in the first place and less polluting to use.

Another preparty step can involve dry-cleaning. Be sure and check the list at *www.greenearthcleaning.com* or at *www.findco2.com* for a dry cleaner near you that uses a more earth-friendly liquid silicone instead of the industrial solvent perchloroethylene. Also, it is a good idea to bring back the wire hangers to your dry cleaner so that they can use them again. Some dry cleaners are switching to a more environmentally friendly pressed paper clothes hanger.

Food and Drink

We talked earlier about the green practice of buying food that is in season and locally grown. It helps support small local farmers and it cuts down on the amount of energy used to truck food all over the place. Fully 25 percent of all the energy used in the country goes toward the food sector. So for all holiday entertaining, make a special effort to find locally produced foods. Each food item in a typical American meal has traveled an average of 1,500 miles to reach your plate. Imagine that. Instead of putting grapes from Chile on a plate to serve as a snack to guests, maybe you could serve them apples from the farmer up the road.

LOCAL, NOT GLOBAL, FOOD

How do you find local food sources? The LocalHarvest Web site (*www.localharvest.org*) is a great source to help you find what is grown in your area and where you can buy it.

Not all of your guests will join you in a glass of organic wine, so what can you serve them other than those small bottles of water? Not only is that an inelegant touch to just hand a party guest a plastic bottle of water, we all know how much excess landfill all those bottles now create. Instead, why not fill a tub of ice with various bottles of organic juices or natural sodas? For tho water drinkers at your party you can fill a pretty pitcher with water that you've already run through a purifying filter such as Brita. Check out their info at *www.filterforgood.com.*

Are those fancy and expensive glass bottles of imported European sparkling water any greener? Perhaps. A case could be made that since the bottle is glass there is a good chance it will be recycled and reused, but it still had to travel quite a distance to reach your party, didn't it?

When Your Meal's a Turkey

Whole Foods Market can come to the rescue if you forgot to defrost your turkey in time or if you want a quick alternative to defrosting it yourself. They sell fully-cooked organic turkeys that can be heated in a matter of hours.

If you're not serving an entire dinner—or if you want to put out something for your guests to nibble on before the main course is served—roasted nuts make a simple and elegant party snack. They also make your house smell wonderful, so wait until just before your guests arrive to quickly roast them. Use organic nuts like almonds, pecans, or walnuts, and toss them with 2 tablespoons of butter and salt and pepper to taste. Chop up herbs like rosemary or sage and add to the tossed nuts. Spread on a baking sheet and roast at 375 degrees for eight minutes or so. Check them frequently to make sure they don't burn.

No-Meat Entertaining

The holidays are also a perfect time to consider lightening up a bit on your meat consumption, if not go meat-free altogether. Karen Shuppert, a nutrition educator in Napa, California, has a practice based on SOUL food—seasonal, organic, unrefined, and local. She suggests the following for an amazing meat-free holiday buffet: "Eating well is all about color, the color of fruits and veggies. Combine lots of colors, for good health and flavor. Holiday season is oranges and reds, dark greens, and yellow citrus too. Your choices can focus on bringing color to the table and to our systems, eating a wide variety of colors gives you the full range of nutrients."

Here's what Karen will be setting out on the buffet for her guests during the holidays:

"Get your reds and oranges from roasted peppers, winter squashes like butternut and kombucha, pumpkin, and sweet potatoes. Don't forget carrots! Getting into the greens, this is a terrific time to do heartier foods

GOBBLE THESE
For festive vegetarian holiday meals check out the turkey alternatives from these companies:

Tofurky Feast:
www.tofurky.com
Quorn Meat-free Roast:
www.quorn.com
Un-Turkey Feast:
www.nowandzen.net

like broccoli, Swiss chard, and kale. Mushrooms are another great winter food. You can enhance your buffet with some of the autumnal fruits like apples and pears and winter fruits like citrus."

Party Decorations

Just like the low-cost, eco-friendly ways we recommended for decorating your house for the holidays, there are many ways to give your home or party space a festive feel without buying more or buying things that can't be reused. Start by looking around to see what you already have. Be creative about incorporating unusual items into your holiday décor—glittery scarves and dangling earrings can be pressed into service to create a glamorous atmosphere. Hang them on the back of a chair or from a lamp fixture.

Here is what the Sander family does. Every year a few nights before Christmas Jennifer hosts a big Pirate Dinner and thoroughly enjoys the process of searching the house for things that can be put to piratey use. Both of her sons, Julian and Jonathan, enjoy the hunt too. Tarnished silver can look very piratelike, as do tangled beads and costume jewelry. Goblets are filled with weird foreign coins. Scraps of velvet and satin and the fake spider web stuff from Halloween create a strange shipwrecked dinner party feel that guests (particularly young ones) enjoy and our family loves to create.

If you don't see anything inspiring around your house, ask someone else if you can borrow party items rather than going out to buy more. Make sure you are only borrowing from the same people you invited. It wouldn't be too nice to ask a friend if you can borrow a big coffeepot only to have to hem and haw when she asks you why you need it.

An inexpensive way to dress up a buffet table for your party is to use large clear glass vessels and fill them with fruits and vegetables like Concord grapes, figs, pomegranates, Brussels sprouts, or citrus fruits. Your decorations will do double-duty, as the money you spend on decorations will also be buying you snack and breakfast food for the next few days, long after your guests are gone!

However you decide to make your house festive, remember to skip one thing — glitter. Just like with glitter encrusted greeting cards, this is not something that can be recycled. And it is a headache to clean up afterwards!

Create your own private club atmosphere by closing the drapes in your main party space. It will help keep heat in the room—think of all those warm bodies that will be milling around—and give your event a cozy feeling. Add to the club atmosphere with dimmer switches and low lighting. Your guests all look better in soft lighting anyway; they will love you for it and won't even suspect that you are trying to go light on the energy use.

Party Night

Encourage all of your guests to rideshare and carpool to your party. Offer to put new friends in touch with each other to share rides. Who knows, you might spark a new romance by whom you pair up! Can they use public transportation to get to your house instead of driving? Maybe you can offer a door prize to the person who used the most creative noncar method of reaching your house.

Put Out the Real Plates

When it comes to serving your guests, please use real plates, silverware, drinking glasses, and cloth napkins. Why? It gets back to the whole thing about waste and landfill and paper use. Just the facts on paper napkins alone are stunning. Americans each use 2,200 paper napkins a year. Can you picture that? We don't just use one at each meal, we use several at each meal. Picture what happens when you go out for fast food; you grab a bunch instead of just one. Making the switch to using cloth napkins at home will help cut down on paper use.

Plastic or paper picnic plates, those little plastic knives and forks, and all those Styrofoam or plastic cups get used once and then tossed into the trash. There is a source of reusable plastic plates (and they are made from recycled plastic!) if you don't have enough actual plates for your party guests; *www.recycline.com* sells PreServe plastic tableware, tumblers, and cutlery that is made from 100 percent recycled plastic and is made in the United States. You can even wash these plastic plates in the dishwasher. Buy them online or at Whole Foods Market and some Target stores.

It's not really so onerous to wash real glassware and silverware. Even Anne's church, long addicted to plastic everything, uses real stoneware for church suppers and real mugs for coffee. Recently glass communion cups even resurfaced. The generation of women who spent Sundays washing up has died, and younger people concerned about the environment have no problem trading a few soapy minutes to avoid needless waste.

Fabikins is a company devoted to the idea of using cloth napkins made from natural fabrics like bamboo and organic cotton. Take a look at what they have to offer at *www.fabikins.com*.

Green Holiday Party Themes

Good parties have themes—it's more fun and gives you a pattern for decorating, entertaining, and even dressing. And it provides for interesting conversation with your guests too.

Organic Winetasting

A great idea for a small gathering is to host an organic winetasting party. You will need to keep it to six or eight guests max for a tasting party. Add organic chocolates and cheeses from local sources to round out the menu.

Is organic wine really drinkable? Roxanne Langer, owner of WineFUNdamentals, tells us that "When I first started in the wine industry twenty-some years ago, there was not a lot to be said for the taste of organic wines. Back then most people who consumed organic wines did so for principle, at least I hope that was their reason as the taste profile of organics was 'spotty' at best. The tide began to swing first in the vineyards as more and more viticulturalists became champions of the soil in their vineyards. Instead of wanting to kill off everything living in the soil with pesticides and fungicides they began to want to 'naturally' nurture without the use of chemical fertilizers."

The country's oldest organic winery is Frey Vineyards. They have been producing organic wines since 1980 and were also the first in the country to produce biodynamic wines. Katrina Frey reminded us that the holidays are a wonderful time to celebrate with organic wines. Full-bodied red wines in particular go with the hearty warm foods of winter and also mix wonderfully with rich desserts. The classic combo is Cabernet Sauvignon with chocolate. "I like a small company called Equal Exchange that does fair trade chocolate as well as organic," she said. "We link to them on our site."

And wine makes wonderful gifts, Katrina points out. "You can make reusable cloth wine bags, and encourage people to reuse the bag. Or what about buying a cool new pair of high-performance athletic socks and putting the bottle inside the socks instead of wrapping? You could say it was to make someone both warm and cozy." Frey is introducing a new dessert wine, Dessertage, just in time for the holidays. Look for Frey wines at your local Whole Foods Market or at *www.freywine.com*.

Okay, you've invited six or eight guests to an organic wine, cheese, and chocolate night, now what? Roxanne teaches wine-tasting techniques at many home settings and was happy to provide pointers on how to hold a winetasting this holiday season:

"Home winetasting parties can be very fun and creative. Once you choose the theme, you can either request every guest to bring a bottle based on your theme or you can select all the wines yourself. So encourage your guests to go out and find organic wines or go to your wine shop and see what they have.

"Your next decision is whether or not you wish to conduct the tasting blind. A blind tasting is where all of the wines are hidden from view. The purpose of a blind tasting is to take away 'perceived perception.' For instance, if you are doing a Cabernet Sauvignon tasting and one bottle is Gallo and the other is the famous Mondavi wine Opus, the majority of people will immediately perceive that the Opus is a much better wine (even before they've tasted it!). However, if you conduct the same tasting blind, you will probably be amazed at the results."

Méthode Champenoise

Organic champagne! Yes! Okay, technically we can't go ahead and call it champagne (because it wasn't grown in the Champagne region in France), but Jeriko in Mendicino, California, was the first winery in the United States to produce sparkling wine crafted from organically grown and certified grapes. If you watch the PBS cooking show *Secrets of a Chef*, with Hubert Keller, you've seen the Jeriko winery as the holiday episode was filmed there. Depending on the year, their Blanc de Blanc Brut runs around $39 and up. Danny Fetzer, the Jeriko founder and winemaker, thinks there is no better way to toast a green Christmas than with an organic sparkling wine. Ask for it at your local wine shop or check their Web site at *www.jeriko.us*.

What goes better with champagne than dessert? The nice folks at Jeriko are friends with the nice folks at Cheesecake Momma (*www.cheesecakemomma.com*), online purveyors of organic cheesecake. You can visit the Cheesecake Momma site and order both an organic cheesecake and the organic Jeriko wine to go with it at

. . . AND NO HANGOVERS

Promise your friends they'll feel better in the morning if they drink organic wine. Yes, it is true. The sulfites used in many nonorganic wines as a preservative can be the reason behind some next-day headaches. One in 100 people is sensitive to sulfites.

the same time! Their organic Chocolate Cheesecake is paired with Jeriko's '05 Cabernet; sounds like a great combo to us. For the holiday season Cheesecake Momma sells an organic pumpkin cheesecake from October through January.

The Local Foods Party

Another green-themed holiday party idea is to invite friends for a "localvore" evening. Localvore? Also sometimes called locavore, the concept refers to eating foods from your local area. Chances are the organic chocolate won't be locally grown, but you will uncover amazing choices once you begin your search. Remember the Web site at *www.localharvest.org* for help in finding area growers.

You might check into having your party at a local organic farm. No doubt they are looking for ways to bring in some more money during the nongrowing season and would love to have something going on in the barn that time of year. It doesn't hurt to ask. Anne Dougherty, who runs the gourmet food travel company Learn Great Foods, tells us that winter is a wonderful time to spend time with local growers. Check into your region's Slow Food organization (*www.slowfoodusa .org*) and see if they have any holiday events happening. It would be a great way to learn more about what is being produced near you by small farmers and growers.

Christmas Book Club

Why not throw a party centered on books? You can form a one-time Christmas book club with a handful of friends. Encourage everyone to read the same book and come prepared to discuss it. Have a potluck dinner, and have everyone bring as a gift a copy of a book that they already own, read and enjoyed, and would be happy to give to someone else to enjoy.

A homemade soup night would be a wonderful way to gather friends and family on a cold winter night during the holiday season. Invite everyone to bring along their own favorite homemade soup, add a salad selection and some fresh bread, and you have a simple supper evening that is low cost, low stress, and doesn't emphasize over-the-top celebration.

Holiday Card Party

This would be a great party for neighbors, friends, and kids of all ages; you can all gather in one spot in early December and make your own greeting cards out of recycled materials. Encourage your guests to bring along more supplies to share, like paper bags, old scraps of construction paper, leftover craft paints, old wallpaper scraps—whatever can be a part of a homemade card. Put it all out and see what you can all make! This would also be an easy way to hold a potluck cookie afternoon; let people know that you will be making a few batches and ask that they bring along a dozen of their family specialty.

Out of Sight, Out of Mind

Not that happy with the way your house looks? Wish you could hide your computer workstation or the kid's toys from view for the night? That is what screens were made for! Look around your house to see if there is something you can turn into a clutter-hiding screen. Chances are you have something out in the garage that can be put to use. Peter and Jennifer fashioned a large room screen out of old cupboard doors. A friend was remodeling her kitchen and replacing the old cupboard doors, so Jennifer asked if she could have a few. A few brass hinges, a bit of paint, and there you have it—a tall Chinese red screen that can be put into service as needed. Do you have old doors that can be hinged together? Be creative!

Green Your Office Party

Holiday office parties tend toward excess. If you've ever had to clean up after one you know exactly what I mean. Mounds of napkins and plates, garbage bags stuffed with bottles and cans, half-eaten cheeses and meat trays that don't fit back into the refrigerator. We're getting worn out just thinking about it!

Be very careful about ordering in quantity, and make arrangements in advance to donate leftovers to a local food bank or shelter. If you don't have time to do that, make it a point to encourage coworkers and guests to take the extra food home.

Cut down on the paper and plastic, and make an effort to use plates and utensils from recycled materials. In addition to the many products available online at *www.recycline.com*, you can order an "office pack" of cups, plates, utensils, and napkins all bundled together for office use and made from renewable products from the Green Event Shop (*www.greeneventshop .com*). Cofounder Nan Leuschel points out that with all the holiday parties there are more opportunities to go green! The Green Event Shop carries packages that could serve a group of up to 200 servings. For a little more, you can create your own custom package of napkins, plates, cups, and utensils to fit the group you are expecting.

When it comes to choosing the location for your office holiday party, try to stick close to the office. If the party is a few miles away, everyone will pile into their own cars and drive individually. Instead of that scenario, is there a restaurant or venue nearby the office where you can all walk? Is there a place you can all reach on public transportation? If not, encourage carpooling to and from the location to eliminate excess driving. Do you give out awards and prizes at the annual holiday party? Why not go green there too:

- The top salesperson could win a carbon offset for his or her air travel from *www.liveneutral.org*
- The employee of the year could win sports tickets or a massage, an experience rather than another useless gizmo or plaque
- Secret Santa traditions are another place to go green—put out an officewide challenge to see who can come up with the best green gift for under $10!

Here is a green step you can institute at the office after the party is over—change the coffee. We know holiday food choices add up. Go with local food sources to make a difference when it comes to fuel use and go with organic to keep pesticide use down, but there is one other choice you can make—try to buy "shade-grown" coffee. If the coffee you drink at home or in the office was grown on clear-cut land, which is most commercial coffee, it has contributed to deforestation. Beans grown under the rain forest canopy preserve trees. Check the label on the coffee you buy. Can you also cut down on paper waste at the office by switching to a gold mesh filter that can be used over and over and over again?

Good sources for shade-grown coffee are the Audubon Coffee Club, at *www.auduboncoffeeclub.com*, and Tree Frog Coffees, at *www.treefrogcoffees.com*. The Audubon folks are involved because coffee plantations have been destroying rain forests in favor of open fields, removing much-needed migratory bird habitat. You can also get some shade-grown coffees at your local Starbucks.

Green Christmas Weddings

Christmas is a romantic time of the year to get married—twinkly lights everywhere, a smile on everyone's lips, and holiday decorations already in place. If you are planning a wedding, go green to keep in the holiday theme! For weddings at home, try to use some of the earlier ideas about decorating and entertaining. If you are planning a large wedding at a hotel or event center, be sure and interview the caterer or hotel about their waste policy (do they donate extras to food banks?) and their recycling policy. If you are planning to have your reception at a local restaurant, you can also check to see if they are a member of the Green Restaurant Association at *www.dinegreen.com*. The association sets standards that members must meet on various environmental guidelines, such as using sustainable food, using non-toxic cleaning products, and the use of green power.

When planning menus for a Christmas wedding reception, also keep in mind what grows that time of year. Not much, actually, so something like a large tomato salad is not going to be locally sourced. Discuss this with the caterer too—ask about whether they use local sources for food and produce.

Make sure your friends know not to toss glitter in the air as you drive off to your new future together. Let your party planners know you would prefer a biodegradable, water-soluble confetti sendoff from a supplier like *www.Ecoparti.com*.

Relax and Have Fun

Parties should be fun. Not stressful, not tense, but relaxed and enjoyable for the guests and the hosts. Use the eco-friendly holiday entertaining tips we shared to create a memorable evening or afternoon for friends and family.

Five Green Entertaining Ideas to Remember

1. Invite your guests with online invitations or hand-made paper cards.
2. Use local food sources and organic wines.
3. Decorate with what you already have or can borrow from friends.
4. Encourage guests to carpool or rideshare.
5. Use real plates, silverware, glasses, and napkins or plastic versions made from recycled plastic.

7. Green Holiday Getaways

Of course you need a getaway. The holidays are a great time to do that. You may or may not have family to visit, but for sure you have some time off work and the kids have time off school. That's the important thing. You and 65 million other Americans take to the road. You and 8 million other Americans take to the skies. Or you take a train, bus, or who knows what—but you want to go somewhere.

That's okay. It's good to get away once in a while. We all need it. It's just that some ways of doing it are greener than others. As we'll see, some travel methods are greener than others. Likewise, some destinations are greener than others.

The High Green Cost of Travel

Travel is important for most of us, and it's important for the economy too. According to the 2007 edition of

Peter's *Cities Ranked and Rated: More than 400 Metropolitan Areas Evaluated in the U.S. and Canada*, approximately 4.1 percent of the average U.S. state's GDP comes from tourism. And not surprisingly, that varies a lot by state—from only 2 percent in Delaware and 2.5 percent in Indiana to 19.4 percent in Nevada and 15.0 percent in Hawaii. No surprises there.

And travel, being largely based on fossil-fuel consuming vehicles, has a sizeable green impact as you might expect. At the UN World Trade Organization's Second International Conference on Climate Change and Tourism in October 2007, delegates agreed that "the tourism sector must rapidly respond to climate change, within the evolving UN framework and progressively reduce its Greenhouse Gas (GHG) contribution if it is to grow in a sustainable manner."

The group went on to suggest actions to ". . . mitigate its greenhouse gas emissions, derived especially from transport and accommodation activities; adapt tourism businesses and destinations to changing climate conditions; and apply existing and new technology to improve energy efficiency."

A report produced by the global travel agency Travelport states that we don't really know how much environmental damage is specifically caused by the tourism industry as a whole. It's hard to measure in part because it's hard to separate the travel in tourism from travel in normal activities of daily life. But Travelport does share some interesting statistics.

One of their studies compares the CO_2 footprint of a rail versus an auto versus an air trip per passenger from London to Edinburgh, Scotland. That 400-mile trip by air would produce 87 kilograms (191 pounds) of CO_2 per person. By car it would produce 115 kg (253 pounds), and by rail, 33 kg (82.5 pounds). Pretty big—and a pretty big difference.

Planes, Trains, and Automobiles

Okay, so the Travelport study lays down the gauntlet. Drive on that holiday trip, especially alone, and your size 13 carbon footprints will be seen and felt for miles. Fly and it isn't so bad, but if there are four of you, why, that might not be the answer either. And don't forget the impact of that thing called "ground transportation," which gets you back and forth to the airplane.

Clearly and not surprisingly, the best way to go on a holiday getaway aside from nonpowered means of conveyance like bicycles or on foot is to go by train. The carbon footprint is less than a third of driving. It could be considered zero, for the train goes anyway, whether you're on it or not. We'll be back to talk more about that one.

Now, Just Automobiles

Naturally, if cars were something we bought and sold during the holidays or for the holidays, we'd be devoting a sizeable section of *Green Christmas* to the selection and purchase of environmentally friendly automobiles. But since the car you own is the one you're probably going to use for that holiday trip, there isn't so much to talk about. Or is there?

A PRIUS, WITH A RED BOW, PLEASE

Suppose Santa *is* bringing you a new car. Log on to Yahoo! Autos Green Center (*http://autos.yahoo.com/green_center/*) for overall green ratings and rankings on factors like fuel economy and greenhouse gas emissions, as well as timely information on really green cars, like hybrids.

As it turns out, regardless of the car you already own, how you maintain and drive it can make a big difference, not just at holiday time, of course, but all the time. And then there's the car you drive that you don't own. No, we're not talking about *Grand Theft Auto*—we're talking about the car you rent if you fly or take the train to that out-of-town destination.

Give Me Some Air, Please

You've heard it before: a clean car runs better. No real reason, except that you feel better and look better in it. Get all the crud off the windshield and tires and floor mats and seats, and it just seems quieter, faster, and, well, newer. But you should also know that a clean air filter gives you better gas mileage and, of course, helps reduces that carbon footprint a tad closer to elf size. How much better mileage? According to the EPA and Department of Energy's shared Fuel Economy Web site (*www.fueleconomy.gov*), a clean air filter can increase your mileage up to 10 percent.

And that's not all. A properly tuned engine can save another 4 percent, and properly inflated tires can save another 3 percent. So before you load up and take off, give your car a little checkup.

Over the River and Through the Woods— Slowly, Please

It makes a lot of difference how you drive your car, too. According to the Fuel Economy Web site, just plain "aggressive" driving—speeding, rapid acceleration, hard braking—can cost you up to a third in fuel economy at highway speeds and 5 percent around town. So, gentle as she goes.

And about speed itself, yes, it does make a difference. Those 55 mph speed limits of days gone by really were about fuel savings, not just giving anxious high-

way patrol folks something to do and a
way to achieve quotas. Again, according to the Fuel Economy site, for a
car capable of getting 30 mpg on
the highway, that level is almost
reached at 30 mph and peaks
between 50 and 55 mph. Then
the forces of wind resistance
take over, and mileage drops to
about 26 mpg at 65 mph and to
about 23 mph at 75 mph. Of course,
it depends on the wind profile of your
vehicle and other conditions, like wind
and how flat the road is.

**STAY OUT
OF THE
FAST LANE**

For those of you who like rules of
thumb, here's a rule of thumb: each 5
miles per hour you drive over 60 is the
fuel efficiency equivalent of adding 20
cents per gallon to your fuel bill.

The site claims that slower speeds will save you 7
to 23 percent in fuel (and emissions), the equivalent to
a gas price difference of 77 to $1.33 cents per gallon
(based on an average gas price of $4.03 per gallon).

Time to Lose Some Weight?

Much is said about avoiding those extra pounds
gained during the holidays, but what about those extra
books and CDs you've been lugging around, meaning to
donate, for weeks now? Sure, you just haven't had time
to do it, but your car still has to do the work to get it all
from one place to another. According to the EPA/DOE,

every 100 pounds of stuff in your trunk costs 1 to 2 percent in fuel economy.

And don't forget to take that roof rack off if you aren't using it (and if you are, consider taking less!). Sure, it makes you look more active and cool, especially if it's a ski, snowboard, or bike rack, but it will cost you 5 percent or so in fuel economy.

Renting Green

Most of us don't think of car rental companies as the most progressive companies on the planet. We're still dealing with "We're #1" and "We Try Harder" long after the demise of "Platformate," as Shell's claim to fame for gasoline, or "It's the Real Thing" for a bottle of Coke.

Be that as it may, there is a movement underfoot to build hybrids into car rental fleets. For the moment, Enterprise Rent-A-Car (*www.enterprise.com*) seems to be leading the way with some 4,000 Toyota Priuses in its fleet. Enterprise recently announced an initiative to put four green branches in Atlanta and to offer a fleet containing some 60 percent fuel-efficient vehicles. Some of the other players—notably Avis and Budget—are cautiously following suit.

And does a daily Toyota Prius set you back as much as a Lamborghini Countach might? Happily, no. Reports suggest it may cost $5 to $15 a day more to rent versus a comparable non-hybrid—$40 for a weekly rental. That's about the same as the extra driver fee or the passenger facility usage charge you pay. (Money-saving hint—ask your way out of the extra driver fee.) At $4 per gallon, it doesn't take too much in gas savings to cover this difference. Of course, you'll leave smaller carbon footprints.

TAXI!
Major cities have been experimenting with hybrid taxis. On this continent, Vancouver, B.C., leads the way with a third of its fleet in hybrids. New York expects its fleet to expand to 1,000 vehicles in 2008 from 315 in 2007. Are fares higher? No—at 50 mpg, the drivers, who normally pay fuel costs, are still coming out ahead while keeping fares where they are.

Eco-Friendly Hotels

Congratulations! You got to where you're going by car, plane, or train. Now, where do you stay? Your hotel can make a difference too. Some are a lot greener than others.

There are no standards today for rating the carbon emissions or other green characteristics of hotels. Several groups, however, are beginning to identify eco-friendly hotels based on specific or sometimes more general criteria. Travel Web sites like Orbitz and Expedia are getting onto the green bandwagon with special green programs covering both hotels and transportation.

Orbitz has, by its own explanation, just "started the process of researching hotels with 'eco-friendly' policies." Their selections are based on hotels having at least one of the following criteria already in place:

- Use a natural source of energy (wind, water, solar, biofuel)
- Use environmentally friendly and safe cleaning and personal products (detergents for linens, soaps, and shampoos)
- Contribute money from each hotel reservation to an environmental organization
- Use of energy conserving devices (eco-friendly light fixtures/bulbs triggered by motion detectors, water-saving devices, water filtration systems, and air filtration/purifiers)
- Earned the ENERGY STAR (*www.energystar.gov*) under guidelines set forth by the U.S. Department of Energy and the Environmental Protection Agency

Orbitz is actively asking hotels whose owners think they qualify to contact them and get onto the program. It's pretty new; at the time of this writing there were twenty-two qualifying hotels in California, twenty in Florida, and fourteen in Arizona. If your holiday plans suggest going somewhere else, check out *www.eco.orbitz.com*.

Green National Parks

Not too surprisingly, some of the newest green hotels and lodges are found in national parks. The most recent national park lodge to open is just outside of San Francisco. Located at Fort Baker in the Golden Gate National Park's Cavallo Point, The Lodge at Golden Gate has taken many strides in the green direction. All suites have organic bedding, and the site has been cited as a premier example of historic preservation. Find more online at *www.cavallo point.com*.

TAKING THE LEED

Seek out green hotels. If your holiday travels take you to San Francisco you can stay in California's first LEED-certified (Leadership in Energy and Environmental Design) hotel, Orchard Garden Hotel (*www .theorchardgardenhotel.com*), built green with the latest green building standards, not just converted to green.

For a more traditional lodge in a more traditional location, there's Signal Mountain Lodge, on the shores of Jackson Lake in Wyoming's Grand Teton National Park. It's a collection of rustic log cabins and larger lakefront retreats. In 2002 it became the first national park concessionaire to become Green Seal Certified, with numerous programs ". . . addressing waste reduction, reuse of goods, recycling, environmentally preferable purchasing, integrated pest management, water quality protection, energy and water conservation, and other issues that affect the resources of Grand Teton National

Park and our planet." Check it out at *www .signalmountainlodge.com.*

GREEN, EH?!

Several green hotel initiatives have their roots in Canada. The Fairmont Hotels Green Partnership program started in the company's Canadian properties in 1990. A Canadian environmental marketing company called TerraChoice has partnered with Audubon International to develop the Green Leaf Eco-Rating System for hotels.

Hold That Towel, Please

By custom and tradition, hotels change all sheets and towels every day. Now that's a good thing when different guests are involved, but if you're staying in the same hotel for several nights, do you really need a complete new set of linens? Think about it—do you change your sheets and towels at home every day? Probably not!

Many hotels have asked the question for years with those little cardstock "tents" in your bathroom (Do you really need new linens? Check here if you don't.). Was the hotel taking this action to be green? Maybe, maybe not. More likely it was an attempt to save laundering costs.

Making the hotel more profitable may not be one of your top objectives, but being green is. So even if you don't have one of the little tents, you can still call housekeeping and advise them that there's no need to change the sheets and the towels daily. This one small gesture, made by enough travelers, can save enormous amounts of water and energy (lots of hot water) and reduce the amount of soapy effluents in the disposal system too.

Give Back Getaways

It's time to switch gears from the nuts and bolts of travel, like planes, trains, automobiles, and hotels, to true green destinations to consider as a special holiday treat for your family. There's some pretty cool new stuff out there.

Where did we get the title Give Back Getaways from? From none other than the crème de la crème of luxury hotels, the venerable Ritz-Carlton chain of hotels. Not only does the Ritz have a green policy, they have also begun a program by that name.

Here's the deal. Not only do you get first-class accommodations in a green-sensitive context, but hotel guests can then sign up to help out on community projects like restoring the Everglades (Palm Beach), work in a food bank (Dallas), or help restore a mountain trail (Half Moon Day). In Colorado, at the Ritz-Carlton Bachelor Gulch, guests can participate in Snowboard Outreach. You can find out what is happening during the holidays at *www.ritzcarlton.com.*

Green Hawaii

Speaking of Hawaii and speaking of green, what could be greener than a Hawaiian tropical island? *Conde Nast Traveler* named the Mauna Lani Resort (*www.mauna lani.com*) one of the "World's Top Earth-Friendly Getaways" in their January 2008 issue. The award-winning Big Island resort, amazingly, is the only beach resort in the United States named in the collection. Mauna Lani has quite an environmental pedigree, starting with the stewardship of a culturally and environmentally sensitive place, an old native fishing ground, along the Kohala coast. Using three acres of photovoltaic cells, it produces more solar power than any luxury resort in the world, providing operating power and the majority of water pumping requirements, which are significant since the resort's two championship golf courses are located in the middle of a black lava desert.

In fact, the resort has been recognized by the EPA and DOE for its accomplishments, particularly in advancing the development of the green power market. Says *Conde Nast Traveler*: "It is estimated that over the twenty-five-

FIRST-CLASS GREEN DESTINATIONS

Hawaii isn't the only place to find a first-class green destination for your holidays. They're all over the world—in the Caribbean, Latin America, the South Pacific, tropical Asia. Check out hotels and resorts with the Rues Hotel Selection (RHS) at *www.ecofriendlyhotelsrhs.com*.

year lifetime of the environmentally friendly system, emissions of carbon dioxide will be reduced by almost 12,000 tons." Green or not, it's a great place to relax and commune with nature.

Ski Holidays

If a tropical green paradise isn't quite on your Christmas holiday list, know that, like the big hotel chains, ski resorts are also greening up their act. In our neck of the northern California woods, the Sierra-at-Tahoe ski resort (*www.sierra-at-tahoe.com*) is getting into the act, as are many other prominent ski resorts.

Sierra-at-Tahoe allows drivers of hybrid vehicles to use the preferential parking area for free (skipping the $15 charge). They use eco-friendly cleaning products, and—get this—each spring they give money-saving coupons for lift tickets to people who dropped off their used electronics at an e-recycle center.

Those of you that ski know that, other than snow, the one thing in abundance at most ski resorts is wind, and wind can be turned into power. Several prominent resorts, including Mount Bachelor in Oregon, Jackson Hole in Wyoming, and Jiminy Peak in Massachusetts, have taken advantage of wind power to power their chairlifts. And if you're sitting on top of a potential volcano, why not take advantage of the geothermal opportunity—

as Mammoth Mountain Resort has done in California's eastern Sierra? Green building projects are also under way at Stowe Mountain in Vermont and Aspen, Colorado.

Organic Food Holidays

Okay, a food holiday might sound closer to your usual Christmas and holiday itinerary, right? Why not wander around in the winter among small wineries and gourmet food growers? As ecotourism combines with a greater interest in farming brought on by world food demand and shortages, we're starting to see some interesting opportunities to eat a lot, learn a lot, and enjoy an almost-forgotten agrarian lifestyle. What a nice holiday treat!

Learn Great Foods — and Other Farm Stuff

"There is nothing so cozy as wandering around visiting a snow-blanketed farmstead," says Ann Dougherty, founder of Learn Great Foods, a Midwest-based "culinary adventure" company. "We love to visit farms during the winter when our farmer friends have time to talk with us. At the end of our All Things Chocolate week-

HOLIDAY BIKING

An active-travel outfit called Backroads (*www.backroads.com*) offers guided biking tours around the world. In December they have trips that let you bike through Vietnam, Cambodia, and around Hawaii's Big Island. You can do a family multisport vacation in Costa Rica that lets you all bike, hike, and kayak. Something for everyone!

end, for example, chef and market gardener Mike Everts whipped up some squash ginger bisque for the group. He never would have had time to do that in the summer! Then we all tromped out into the snowy fields to look for carrots. Frost sweetened carrots were amazing." Learn Great Foods offers Culinary Retreats and Culinary Farm Tours. They visit organic farms and food artisans of all kinds in the United States and Latin America. For instance, in February of 2009 they will repeat the popular All Things Chocolate weekend in Petoskey, Michigan. You can find their tour schedule at *www.learngreatfoods .com*. "We love selling gift certificates!" Ann tells us.

NO GPS, BUT IT'LL DO

How do you find the groovy green places when traveling? You can use a green map that shows you where to find farmers markets, hiking spots, and other green-focused things. Try *www.greenmap.org*.

Convive with Your Food

Intrigued with Learn Great Foods? There's a larger movement afoot, known as slow food. Okay, follow along with us, here. There's an organization known as Slow Food USA, dedicated to the "taste, tradition, and honest pleasures of food." With us so far?

Slow Food USA is divided up into local chapters, called "convivia." For those of you with limited Latin, a *convivium* comes from the Latin word *convivere*, which means "to live with, hence to feast with." (We didn't make this up, by the way—it comes from the Slow Food USA Web site at *www.slowfoodusa.org.*) There are more than 170 convivia all over the United States. They invite members to "taste, celebrate, and champion the foods and food traditions important to their communities." The convivia host events, many of which are feasts or festivals drawing on locally grown foods.

It's an interesting way to commune with nature, enjoy food, and enjoy special American traditions, all bundled into one. A convivium event might cost $50 to $100 but will provide lasting memories—and probably a new set of friends too.

Time to Cruise?

One of Jennifer's longtime friends has devoted herself to spreading the message of garbage, particularly what happens to garbage on the high seas when cruise ships are afloat. Here is what television producer and writer Kit Dillon Givas thinks you should know before you book that Christmas cruise:

"Lots of people love to avoid the Christmas chaos for one reason or another and book themselves on a cruise. Cruisers love the never-ending view of the beautiful blue waters and the sunsets while out at sea. Not to mention those mile-long buffets that seem to never empty. So where does all that food go? Where do the bath-water, laundry, and dishwashing waters get dumped? And if each passenger goes to the bathroom an average of four times a day while on a seven-day cruise, is that fish food? How about all that fuel a cruise ship uses during just one of its many excursions? Why, out to sea of course!

TAKE THE GREEN TOUR

Ecotourism has been around for a while, and if you search high and low, you'll find lots of green travel services and travel opportunities with altogether green purposes too. A couple of specialized green travel portals come to mind: *www.responsibletravel.com* and another called RezHub at *www.rezhub.com*.

"Since people starting exploring the world by ship there has been dumping into the sea. Cruise ships give people the chance to see the world, make friends, and float on pristine waters, and millions of people do each and every year.

"The Clean Cruise Ship Act of 2005 (S793/HR1636) was enacted to regulate cruise ship practices and to stop them from discharging sewage, gray water, and oily bilge water within twelve miles of the eastern shores and in the Great Lakes. California and the Hawaiian Islands only have a three-mile offshore dumping provision.

"Alas, most cruise lines are registered in foreign countries that do not have to adhere to U.S. environmental regulations. There have been monetary fines imposed and millions have been paid, but this continues each and every day. Federal laws are more stringent than local laws that may allow the discharge of treated sewage anywhere. Before you book yourself on a relaxing cruise, ask the company about their policies. And check out *www.bluewaternetwork.org*."

Lastly, you might heed the holiday advice of artist Cathleen Swanson, who suggests that since so many of us find trips to visit family during Christmas to be so stressful, "Maybe we should all stay home and get to know our neighbors better. That would be better for the environment, and better in the long run for our communities."

Of Service to Others

It doesn't cost anything to be of service to others. No gifts to wrap, and a wonderful personal sense of the true meaning of Christmas is yours. Look around in your own neighborhood for opportunities to help out. Or check out *rezhub.com*, mentioned in the sidebar on the previous page. For those of you with time on your hands, RezHub offers a special page called the Volunteer Travel Hub (*www.rezhub.com/VolunteerTravel.aspx*) dedicated to volunteer travel opportunities—chances to travel somewhere for the good of people, animals, or the environment. Now there's a real green way to spend Christmas!

Five Green Holiday Getaway Ideas

1. For long or short distances, train travel is best.
2. Tune your car and remove excess weight to get the best mileage.
3. Ask the hotel or cruise line about its environmental policy.
4. Hybrid rentals cars are available from several major companies.
5. Explore local food-oriented tours during the holidays.

8. Gifts to Reduce, Reuse, and Recycle

All the world loves a gift, and making someone else's face light up is a gift beyond measure. There are steps we can take to prevent this heartfelt human impulse from turning into wasteful one-upmanship. Let's find ways to give that aren't aggressive and obligating. We can start by resolving not to give so indiscriminately that gifts mean nothing.

Does Green Mean Stingy?

For starters, green, like simple, doesn't necessarily mean stingy, cheap, or tight. When you stop and think about it, there are lots of ways to do something fun, original, whimsical, practical, inexpensive, and green. Many of these "simple" gifts will be more used—and more cherished—than the traditional holiday standbys.

Anne's son Alex is an excellent gift giver. Given enough time to think about the recipient, he can come up with something creative and thoughtful—like the Tonka truck he once filled with M&Ms for a girlfriend who loved candy. Expensive? No. And a good reuse for an old Tonka truck and something to smile about for years to come. When your list is longer than your imagination, try giving everyone the same gift:

- Every year Anne gives her former father-in-law and nephews a six-pack of beer in bottles. Everyone gets a different brand—either an interesting import or a new microbrew label.
- One year, Alex was moved to buy cheese for his dad's family. He had a great time searching out unique flavors and brands for members of his family.
- After Anne's friends Carolyn and Rick moved from Manhattan to a "holler" in Virginia, they started making jam from berries on their property. It's something they can do in a couple of afternoons, and it's not costly to mail the jars to everyone on their Christmas list. Anne always looks forward to the arrival of her annual jar!

Shop Green, Give Green

Many large retailers and manufacturers are embracing the green concept, not only to connect with their customer and give them what they want but to have a dramatic and positive effect on their bottom line. Retail juggernaut Wal-Mart has taken several actions to green up their act. They aren't quite there yet though, as CEO Lee Scott, Jr. admitted at a business conference in the spring of 2008. "I haven't a clue," he said, when asked how the company could ever meet his stated goal of having zero waste and 100 percent renewable energy. But they continue to try.

Wal-Mart is making strides in some areas by looking into ways to reduce the amount of plastic used in making bottled-water containers and working with suppliers to reduce excess packaging. According to the *Minneapolis/St. Paul Business Journal*, they are also working with local vendors of environmentally friendly products and services in a move to work with more local companies on sustainability efforts.

If we all decide to seek out organically produced products or green gifts, will that have any real impact on what actually gets sent to the stores? Won't the shelves still be cluttered with stuff that was mass-produced in China and shipped thousands of miles? Personal choices do matter. Just like the way our votes all add up to elect one candidate, a whole lot of individual choices about what we are buying add up to the way the market responds. If the sales of cheap stuff from China fall off, the company that produces it will start asking why. If they learn that consumers have decided to skip their product because they are suspicious of the ingredients or don't like the fact that it was made far, far away, if they want to stay in business they will begin to make changes. It is as simple as that.

How to Reduce

Reducing our overall consumption is one major way we can cut down on energy use. We know it's tough to do at this time of year, but here's something to ponder about the "stuff" that arrives beautifully wrapped and tied with a bow for Christmas: The American Society of Interior Designers (ASID) reports that for every truckload of goods manufactured, thirty-two truckloads of waste are produced. In fact, according to ASID, 90 percent of everything manufactured in this country ends up in landfills within one year.

That fact is prominently mentioned in the short video *Story of Stuff*, which should be required watching for everyone contemplating Christmas shopping. You can find it at *www.storyofstuff.com*. This twenty-minute online film is a real eye opener when it comes to understanding the connection between what we buy and what happens to the environment. Check it out. Watch it with your kids.

Buy What? Buy Nothing?

There are organizations that truly believe that the proper holiday response is to buy nothing. Adbusters (*www.adbusters.org*), the organizers of Buy Nothing Day, which is held the day after Thanksgiving (you know, the same day hoards of people camp out in the parking lot of the mall for the early morning mall opening), put it this way: "Buy Nothing isn't really about refusing to spend a dime over the holiday season. It's about taking a deep breath and deciding to opt out of the hype, the overcrowded malls, and the stressful to-do lists. It's about reminding ourselves to really think about what we are buying, why we are buying it, and whether we really need it at all." If you think you don't need anything at all from anyone, you can go to their site and download Holiday Gift Exemption Vouchers that you can print out and give to the folks that you don't want purchased presents from. Buy Nothing Christmas is an initiative started by Canadian Mennonites but is "open to everyone with a thirst for change and a desire for action." You can download a free information kit at *www.buynothingchristmas.org*.

And lastly, Reverend Billy, of *www.rev billy.com*, is the self-appointed head of a movement of his own making—the Church of Stop Shopping. His new movie, *What Would Jesus Buy?*, is available on DVD.

Take the time to visit a few of these thought-provoking sites before you draw up your annual Christmas list. You might well do it in an entirely different way!

> ### USE LESS STUFF!
> For several years there has also been a Use Less Stuff Day the Thursday a week before Thanksgiving. Founded by the same folks who wrote the book *Use Less Stuff*, Robert Lilienfeld and William Rathje, you can celebrate by focusing on how you too can use less stuff in your life. Find details for this year at *www.use-less-stuff.com*.

Gifts Without the Gift Wrap

Remember from Chapter 1 about the 25 million tons of excess waste generated during the holidays? A great way to cut down on sending wrapping paper to the landfill is simply not to give gifts needing wrapping of any sort. Instead give gifts such as event tickets, gift cards, travel plans, outings, charitable donations, or magazine subscriptions, particularly to green-focused magazines like *Mother Earth News* or *Plenty*.

Another idea is to give memberships in organizations like Co-op America (*www.coopamerica.org*), which sends a copy of the National Green Pages along with a membership. A membership in Slow Foods USA, an organization that works to preserve and protect local foods and traditions, also lets you belong to your local area's Slow Food convivium. You'll find nationwide information at *www.slowfoodusa.org*. (See Chapter 7.)

Perhaps you can create a bird lover, and send someone out into the wilds with a bird-watching book and a promise to accompany them on their first excursion. Check into nature conservancies and preserves in your area and plan an entire day's outing, picnic included. You can also do the same thing with a guide to local hiking trails. Add a pair of thick hiking socks (you can put the book inside the socks and skip the wrapping altogether!) and a homemade coupon promising to hike alongside.

Here are a few other nonthing gift ideas:

● One woman whose family rarely gets together scheduled three family outings for the year ahead. In the winter, everyone met for an evening at a bowling alley. In the spring, they played miniature golf. In the summer, they attended a minor-league baseball game. All three generations enjoyed it.

- Make a donation in someone's name instead. Anne and Alex "buy" animals from the Heifer Project (*www.heifer.org*) for everyone. For Alex's Polish relatives, they choose animals that will go to a project in Poland. For Anne's littler nieces and nephews, they choose fuzzy lambs or bunnies, or a project from a country one of us has visited.
- Anne's friend David gives his children coupons for personally delivered massages. They can't wait to cash them in; however, they see their dad fairly often, so cashing the coupon is easy. Anne's friend Joanne is still holding a coupon for a coffee date that Anne gave her when she moved back from France six years ago. Both women are too busy!
- Another family is pulling together a cookbook of favorite recipes, each one accompanied by a few lines from its contributor explaining how she got the recipe and when she prepares the entrée.

Giving Fewer Gifts—Family Style

One year Anne vowed to turn her collection of old jeans, representing about ten years of wardrobe for Anne and her son Alex, into potholders for everyone she knew. It was a fabulously green idea that never got off the drawing board because, for a casual seamstress with little time for crafts, too much labor was required.

If all she had to do was make one potholder, she might have finished the project. That's the genius of the Christmas gift grab bag, a common bag from which everyone selects just one gift. A grab bag is very green in the sense that it restrains runaway Christmas giving. But lots of people see them as generic and impersonal, and for small children they're a real disappointment.

Personalize Gifts

One large family, with ten grown children and twenty-three grandchildren, personalizes the grab bag concept by holding a drawing at the end of every Christmas celebration. Each adult member draws the name of another adult family member and then spends the next eleven months preparing a gift for that person. The next Christmas everyone gets a present that was made, assembled, or purchased with the tastes and needs of that person in mind. The same family also circulates a painting called *Santa around the World*—originally a vast blue canvas with the tail end of Santa's sleigh visible in the bottom corner. Whoever earns the right to display it for a year must add something to it before passing it on the next year. Now the collage's photo of Mt. Kilimanjaro, African fabric swatches, a rainbow, a pair of wedding rings, and a Macy's Thanksgiving Day parade balloon carry the family's collective memories.

Giving to Others

Americans gave $6.87 billion in online charitable gifts—that is, gifts on behalf of others—in 2006, an increase of 51 percent from 2005. More and more we are accustomed to the idea that someone might give a donation in our name instead of giving us one more gift we probably don't need. There are wonderful places to go online and give a donation in honor of someone. Here are some of our favorites:

- *www.heifer.org*—Help end hunger and poverty around the world. You can choose to fund small projects in countries like Zambia, China, the Ukraine, or Nepal.
- *www.oxfamamericaunwrapped.com*—Invest in a fair trade cooperative or help support a small farmer.
- *www.greengrants.org*—Provides small grants to grassroots environmental groups around the world.

If you still feel you need to hand someone something tangible, a nice way to give a green and loving gift would be to package a small gift with a charitable promise. Give a small gift of organic goat cheese along with a note about giving a gift in honor of the giftee to the Heifer Project, or perhaps a loaf of locally baked bread along with a message about a gift to a hunger organization.

Giving Your Time at the Right Time

Volunteering is a wonderful thing to do, but—bet you didn't think of this—it is better to commit to assisting after the holidays. A friend of Anne's thought it would be a great idea to have her family help serve a holiday meal, so she called a prominent Chicago homeless ministry. The staff person gently suggested something else. "How about calling us in March?" he asked. "Everybody ignores us eleven months of the year, and then they want to show up on Thanksgiving and Christmas." So, great, donate your labor, but schedule it for another time of year.

How to Reuse

You've seen how and why we all need to reduce, but how can we all reuse during the holidays? Used stuff sounds so . . . so tacky. But wait, it's so not tacky! There are countless ways to reuse things that will leave your friends and family in awe of your creative genius.

Instead of making something, you already have something perfect that should be handed on to someone else. "Family heirlooms should be given away at Christmas," our French friend Marie says. Do you have family antiques or objects with sentimental value that should be passed on to someone else? If you have it stuffed in an attic or jammed in a closet, it is time to let someone else appreciate it. Opening a gift of a treasured family piece on Christmas morning will make a far greater impact than something from a store.

Is there a hobby or sport in which you're no longer active? Can you hand your things over to someone else to use them? Pass that fancy racing bike hanging in your garage on to the friend who has long admired it, or give your hiking poles to someone along with a hiking trails book. Peter no longer uses his professional camera equipment much and just offered his tripod to someone else who could use it. That's one less thing in his closet to gather dust, and one less expensive thing she has to buy as she sets herself up professionally.

Freecycling

Around the world there are folks who are willing to give you things for free. Why? Because they don't need it anymore and they don't want to just toss it in the trash. It's called "freecycling," and it is all about reusing and keeping perfectly good things out of the landfill. Membership is free, and there are 4,320 registered groups so there is probably one near you!

Check it out at *www.freecycle.org* and see what is being offered near you. On the other hand, you can also use it to rid yourself of things that you don't want or need anymore, like that old couch you've been dragging around since college. Somebody else needs it, they really do. Jennifer recently checked the local freecycle group near her and found that a bread machine, a large gas BBQ, and a pair of computer speakers were all being offered free to the members. She listed a pair of outgrown children's skis and hopes that someone else will need those, and soon.

Will you find anything through freecycling that will pass muster as a Christmas gift? It is worth a look.

How to Recycle

Some years ago Jennifer was on the verge of tossing out an old wool sweater that some moths had grown too fond of. Just as she was about to drop it into the garbage can, a light bulb went off. Wait! What if she cut off the ribbed turtleneck part of the sweater, did a bit of hemming, and turned it into a cozy warm headband for hiking and skiing? Yes! And if she snipped off the arm that didn't have moth holes in it, knotted the wrist part, and hemmed the edges of the large end, it could be a cute little baby hat! More than one expectant mother has received a baby hat from Jennifer in the past few years.

BACK AND FORTH

Anne and Jennifer have been passing a Norwegian ski sweater back and forth since high school, a relic from their parents' years of living abroad. Is there something you have that someone else has always wanted? Maybe it is time to hand it over on a long-term loan. Perhaps you have under-used clothing, appliances, or bikes that a friend could share.

Ever since then she looks closely at old clothes for ways to make them into other things—old jeans are kept in a bag to use as patches for the boys' jeans, old cotton men's summer shirts are cut up and turned into funky madras and seersucker pillows, and another old fuzzy sweater became a pillow. Our lives are filled with useful things that can be turned into other useful things if we open our minds to the challenge. Before you log on or head out to do Christmas shopping, look closely to see if there is anything you can make from what you already have.

ReadyMade magazine is a totally hip place to look for ideas on how to reuse by turning one thing into another thing. Just like Jennifer's ski headband from an old sweater, these folks can show you how to turn old skateboards into a headboard for a kid's bed, buttons into a mosaic street address plaque, or soda bottles into chandeliers. Too cool. Another great place to find ideas and links to cool reused products is at *www.crafting agreenworld.com*.

Turn Cardboard into Chairs

Does your child need a new chair, stool, or rocker? Stay away from furniture stores and make it yourself out of old cardboard! You can find the plans for these sturdy pieces of furniture at *www.foldschool.com*. Once you figure out how to fold and use cardboard, who knows what you might be able to design and build yourself?

Make Your Own Beeswax Candles

Not only is beeswax a natural wax, the candles burn cleaner, don't produce soot, and burn longer than artificial wax candles. Rolling your own candles out of sheets of beeswax is the easiest way to make handmade candles and make lovely holiday gifts. Even young children can handle this simple process. Jennifer and Peter's sons Julian and Jonathan have been making candles for years and get a big kick out of pointing to a long elegant wax taper and telling dinner guests, "I made that!" You can wrap two (or more) candles with elegant lace ribbon tied in a bow. Sacramento Beekeeping Supplies (*www .sacramentobeekeeping.com*) sells the flat sheets and other supplies online, and there are probably similar stores in your area. Also check out BetterBee (*www

.*betterbee.com*) and Candle Bee Farm (*www.candlebeefarm.com*).

Herbal Fire Starter

It's always nice to have something fragrant—and effective—to start that cozy holiday fire with. Here's the recipe for an herbal fire starter. Lay out a single sheet of newspaper. In the center, mound a few pine cones, a handful of dried herbs like rosemary and sage, or even cinnamon sticks. Roll the paper up around the herbs like you were making a firecracker and tie off both ends with twine. No plastic twine or rope, use cloth or hemp, something burnable. You can also use leftover scraps of wool or cotton yarn.

WRAP AND REWRAP

Here is how to wrap presents using the reuse and recycle concept—an empty cereal box makes a fun gift box for a small child's toy or several books. You can also make simple reusable gift bags out of cloth remnants. You can insert drawstrings and use these bags over and over and over again.

Delivered to Your Door

Ordering online eliminates a driving trip to the mall, and the delivery services just might be the greener option anyway. According to the *Christian Science Monitor*, UPS has purchased fifty hybrid vehicles for short-haul deliveries, which will help it cut emissions by 457 metric tons of carbon dioxide. FedEx is also operating seventy-five hybrids for short-haul deliveries.

UPS examined their routes and realized that much time and fuel was wasted as their drivers sat in the left turn lanes waiting, and waiting, and waiting . . . so they redrew the routes to drive the route counterclockwise and make more right-hand turns. Bingo! They could do the route faster and used less fuel. Is there a way you can drive your usual city routine with more right-hand turns instead of left? Give it a try!

Great Green Gifts Online

The Web is full of sites that sell gifts made from recycled materials, organic and nontoxic materials, and other green gifts. Here are a few of our favorites:

- New York Botanical Gardens Shop (*www.nybgshop .org*)—great green stuff for gardeners and plant lovers
- VivaTerra (*www.Vivaterra.com*)—extremely cool handmade products like carved wooden bowls and jewelry that will delight anyone
- Sundance (*www.sundancecatalog.com*)—lots of products made from recycled materials: bookends made from old railroad ties, felt slippers with soles made from old tires
- Frog Hollow Farm (*www.froghollow.com*)—check out the organic fruit of the month club; you can give someone the gift of healthy fruit all year long

- Global Girlfriend (*www.globalgirl friend.com*)—specializes in green items made by women for women
- A Greater Gift (*www.agreat ergift.org*)—has green and fair trade gifts
- Giggle Fish (*www.gigglefish. com*)—hip and eco-friendly
- Hugger Mugger (*www.hugger mugger.com*)—mind, body, spirit yoga-related gifts

WHAT IS "FAIR TRADE"?

It sounds good, but what is it? You may have seen it at Starbucks and heard about it elsewhere. It's actually an "alternative" code of values, principles, and practice targeted mainly to help disadvantaged trading partners and specified by the International Fair Trade Association (IFAT, *www.ifat.org*).

BOGO It—Buy One, Give One

Another socially conscious concept coming into the foreground is that of BOGO, which stands for buy one, give one. The idea is that you buy something for yourself or a friend, and at the same time you pay extra so that the same item can be given to someone who needs it but can't afford it.

Check out *www.bogolight.com*. Buy one of these amazing-looking flashlights, and the company will donate one as well. A solar panel strip on the side charges in eight hours. Great for your emergency kit.

Also take a look at *www.tomsshoes.com*. These Argentine-inspired slip-on shoes do double duty: buy a pair for yourself and they will donate a pair to a child in need.

VEGGIE GARDEN

Get someone started with a vegetable garden for Christmas. Stash seed catalogs, gloves, and a trowel in their stocking, along with a coupon promising to help with the weeding. Or, get your neighborhood together during the holidays and plan a community vegetable garden to share when the weather turns warm.

Shopping Tips to Save Energy

Let's be realistic: At some point during the months of November and December you will probably get into the car and head to a store. You know what? Although Anne will take the "El" in Chicago, Peter and Jennifer probably will use a car once or twice too. So how can we make sure that the trips we are taking aren't expanding our carbon footprints? A couple of easy things to keep in mind: Planning an afternoon trip to the mall during the holidays? Try to round up a few friends, make an afternoon of it, and carpool! Draw up a long-range plan and try to get your shopping done in one big trip rather than several small ones, or combine the shopping trip with something else. Jennifer and Peter would go out for a special holiday dinner at a nice restaurant in the mall (yes, there are a few) once a year to celebrate. The hour they might have otherwise spent on dessert and an after-dinner drink was spent instead buying the season's gifts for their boys. It saved a trip, saved on the desserts, and gave them something fun to talk about at dinner too.

And for those of you not accustomed to taking public transit on a regular basis, what fun it might be to try a bus or light-rail day for your Christmas shopping, perhaps with downtown shopping as a destination? You'll save fuel, avoid traffic, and share the holiday spirit with other riders, and the necessity of carrying it all might turn you into just a bit more frugal a shopper, right? And, you might discover that the public transit mode isn't so bad for nonholiday shopping, a trip to the museum, or other entertainment either.

HAPPY EMPLOYEES?

Fair trade is about not taking advantage of the disadvantaged. What about employees in all those far-flung places that make your Christmas stuff (if you aren't buying "made in USA" to begin with)? Not sure if you are buying from a company that treats its employees well? Look them up on *www .sweatshopwatch.org.*

Bag Those Shopping Bags

Whole Foods Market has stopped providing shoppers with plastic bags, and many countries are on the verge of taxing plastic bags or banning them outright. It makes sense: why extract resources from the earth for an item you will use for ten minutes?

You've been bringing your own bags to the grocery store for some time now, haven't you? So why not bring your own bags to the mall too? It's easy; just fold up a few of your oversized department stores shopping bags, the ones with the strongest handles, and bring them along. Imagine the look on the clerk's face at Victoria's Secret when you say, "No thanks, I don't need a bag," and slip your just-purchased silk nightgown into a Crate and Barrel bag! Or put the linen napkins you bought for your mom at Crate and Barrel into a Godiva Chocolate bag.

KEEP THOSE BAGS!

Anne and Jennifer's mother bought several large, shiny, red gift bags some years ago and each year at Christmas puts the grandchildrens' gifts inside and sets them in front of the tree. Once the gifts have been removed, she puts the bags back on the shelf for the next Christmas.

And speaking of bags, whenever anyone gives you a present inside of a nicely decorated paper gift bag, fold it up and save it for the next time you have to give someone else a gift and use it a second time. Encourage that person to use it again, and again, and someday perhaps there will only be a few gift bags in circulation being reused by millions!

Almost every grocery store nowadays will sell you a cloth bag with its logo on the side that you can use week after week after week. Are department stores far behind? Not too far. Macy's introduced a $3.95 cloth, 100 percent natural, Macy's shopping bag for Earth Day. Fingers are crossed that they are still there when you walk through the door for holiday shopping.

Sources for reusable shopping bags:

- *www.baggubag.com*
- *www.bringitinabag.com*
- *www.bhappybags.com*

NOURISH, BURN, REUSE

Michael Braungart, the author of *Cradle to Cradle*, a sustainable design book, offers a good way to evaluate possible purchases: "Try to buy stuff that can nourish the earth as compost, burn cleanly as fuel, or return to industry for reuse."

DVD Stocking Stuffers

As you know, we don't want you to browbeat your family and friends with the green philosophy. But if you feel like slipping something with a message into a certain someone's stocking, here are a few to try:

- *Living with Ed*—Season 1 on HGTV
- *The Story of Stuff*
- *An Inconvenient Truth*

. . . or almost anything from Green Planet Films (*www.greenplanetfilms.org*).

Where Does It Say "December 25 Only"?

Does everything have to be celebrated on the same darned day? Do all gifts have to be opened at once? Instead of giving or receiving gifts on Christmas, you can space them out. One woman Anne knows starts giving gifts at Thanksgiving. In mid-December she invites her grandchildren over to bake and reads stories to them. A few days later they spend the night and she gives them new pajamas.

The Danes celebrate Little Christmas Eve on December 23 with a meal followed by carols around the tree. In New York City, a second Christmas shopping season starts December 26, when Dominicans and Puerto Ricans take advantage of after-Christmas sales to stock up for Three Kings Day, a.k.a. January 6 or Epiphany.

Not everything has to be celebrated at the same time of day either. One lovely older woman with a big family no longer invites them for Christmas dinner. There are simply too many of them, and her grown children want to spend the holiday morning with their kids. So she has them over for dessert on Christmas night. She doesn't have to cook a big meal, and everyone looks forward to an evening—instead of a whole day—at Grandma's.

Whatever You Buy, Buy Smart

We will end the green shopping section with a reminder to buy American. Not only can our economy use the boost, but most of the cool recycled and green products are coming from our shores anyway. You'll reduce transportation costs and pollution, especially if you avoid China, one of the more environmentally unfriendly economies.

Whichever way you go—green gifts, charitable gifts, reused gifts (and we are guessing you will do a combination of all three)—rest assured that the shopping decisions you make every day during this holiday season will have a dramatic impact on our world and on what the retail market ends up looking like in the years and decades to come.

Ask any retailer, large or small, some of these questions: Is this made out of organic material? Is this made out of recycled material? Do you donate any portion of your proceeds to charity? Do you work with local suppliers or manufacturers? The more often they hear these kinds of questions, the more often they are likely to realize that, oops, they just lost a sale because you decided to spend your green dollars elsewhere, and the sooner the business world will make the appropriate changes. Dollars spent smart speak loudly.

Five Green Gifting Ideas to Remember:
1. The perfect gift might be an experience to share.
2. Much of what we give ends up in landfills.
3. Look around to see if you already have something that can be given to someone else who wants it.
4. Seek out gifts made from recycled goods and close the loop.
5. Buy American; support your local economy!

Conclusion: Living Green Year Round

By now, we hope you're well on your way to enjoying a wonderful green holiday season. Simple changes, large and small, will make this and all Christmases to come ones to remember.

Can we hang our green-spirited hats on just one season of the year? Sure, we suppose we could, just as religious "C and Eers" faithfully observe their faith twice a year on Christmas and Easter. Naturally, we think there's more to it than just being a "Christmas G"—Christmas green person. Once you've become green at Christmas, why not do it year round? Think of it as an ongoing present to your family, families in the world around you, and future generations.

Developing Green-Eyed Habits

We want to leave you with the final notion that green is a mindset, a set of behaviors, an approach to daily living. It isn't just a set of specialized products and labels. It isn't just stuff you buy. Green is what you do on a daily basis. It's how you make choices between activity A and activity B, between product A and product B. Your ultimate goal is to do what's right. That means doing what's right for the planet, what's right for you and your family, and, ultimately, what's right for your pocketbook, which involves consuming less, consuming smart, and leaving smaller footprints.

It's impossible to cover all there is about going green year round in one concluding chapter. That's really another book, one which has been already written in several forms. The best and most recent treatment of the green topic as a year-round whole is David Bach's *Go Green, Live Rich: 50 Ways to Save the Earth and Get Rich Trying* (Broadway Books, 2008). We can't approach Bach's year-round advice and suggestions in a single chapter.

As an after-dinner palate cleanser, we offer the following ideas to think about. Most involve your home, car and transportation, and daily consumption activities through the year.

Green Your Living Space

How much of our energy use goes toward buildings? Simple answer: a lot. Some 43 percent of the nation's

CO_2 emissions come from energy used to keep us warm or cool, turn on the lights, and power equipment and appliances in our homes and offices. Believe it or not, it's a bigger slice of the pie than the 32 percent of CO_2 that is generated by transportation. In case you're doing the math or just wondering, the rest—25 percent—is produced by industry.

This brings up an interesting point. Even small changes in behavior, if implemented by many people, will have significant consequences. Changing a light bulb may seem small, but multiply that by everyone who uses light bulbs and it's a lot. International travelers may be putting out millions of tons of CO_2 on their jaunts around the world, but there are far more people lighting their homes with light bulbs than there are flying on airplanes. The point is this: the little stuff counts, too, and often counts for more. Especially if it leads to permanent change.

LEEDing the Way

Let's start big—how big *is* Santa's bag, anyway? Living in a greener house would be a huge green present for your family and its future. An organization known as the U.S. Green Building Council has a green certification program known as LEED—Leadership in Energy and Environmental Design Green Building Rating System. LEED is fast becoming a third-party certification not unlike the Underwriter's Laboratories certification of electrical products or the American Dental Association's blessing of toothpastes. New home construction, to get the LEED seal of approval, must meet a lengthy laundry list of requirements.

LEED certification got its start in commercial buildings but is gradually moving into the residential sector. LEED-certified homes, not surprisingly, are more expensive but are also more desirable. Clearly they will save on your utility bills, but they will also fetch a higher resale value and will be eligible for tax credits depending on the state. In New Mexico a Silver LEED-certified 2,000-square-foot house that is at least 40 percent more energy efficient than one built to the standard code can receive a $10,000 tax credit (source, New Mexico Energy, Minerals, and Natural Resources Department).

What's That—a Tax Credit?

The idea of tax credits and incentives for green homes and home improvements is gaining momentum but is hardly universal. Finding the tax credit that applies to your home or home improvement in your state can be pretty tricky. Of course, your builder and supplier of green-friendly hardware can help. There is a handy Web site maintained by North Carolina State University

KITCHEN RECYCLING

Some home remodelers are calling in organizations that remove old cabinets and appliances, then sell the used kitchen parts for less to another homeowner. Check out *www.islandgirlsalvage.com*, *www. driftwoodsalvage.com*, or *www. greendemolitions.org*.

known by the clumsy name Database of State Incentives for Renewables and Efficiency. Clumsy name, but it has a handy nickname: DSIRE. The full URL is *www.dsireusa.com*. And if you want to know more about the New Mexico LEED building credit, check out *www.dsireusa .org/library/includes/incentive2 .cfm?Incentive_Code=NM15F& state=NM&CurrentPageID=1&RE= 1&EE=1*. Okay, we didn't say these credits would be easy to find.

Going green in your home, if it isn't the smart thing to do at today's cost of energy and emissions, will doubt-less become smart in the not too distant future. But there are other reasons, many of which will affect your own personal bottom line. You know what got author David Bach started on his quest for green, which led to *Go Green, Live Rich*? It was the realization that the green-built New York building he makes his home in actually helped with his and his son's allergies.

One Room at a Time

If changing your entire house is not in the budget plan, what about just one room? How about starting with your bedroom, where you spend so much time. We spend so much of our lives sleeping, wouldn't it be better if we weren't all lying down on mattresses that were manufactured with chemicals like formaldehyde, styrene, butadiene, and other petroleum derivatives? Consider these small changes:

- *Organic pillow.* A number of different types and prices are available from *www.savvyrest.com.*
- *Organic sheets and blankets.* Skip chemically-treated sheets and go for the organically-grown variety. All-natural wool is a warm and cozy change you deserve. Check out *www.savvyrest.com.*
- *Organic mattress.* A large investment, to be sure, but what is the point of changing your sheets if you are still lying on a mattress that isn't green? Check out *www.theorganicmattressstore.com*; they deliver anywhere in the United States.

Take the Green Route

Can we walk and bike our way to a better world? It's a good place to start, and it is a wonderful thing to do for your body in these days of ubiquitous obesity. A study by the U.S. Department of Transportation discovered that fully a quarter of all trips we take are less than a mile and that three-quarters of those short trips are taken by car. What we're calling for now is to walk a little farther, maybe a full mile or at least a quarter or half mile. Can you do that? At least some of the time? Of course you can.

Check Out Your Walk Score

There's an interesting new Web tool that scores your home—or your place of work—for walkability. Just enter your address at *www.walkscore.com* to find your score. Here's how the scores work:

- *90–100. Walker's paradise.* Most errands can be done on foot, don't need a car.
- *70*–90. *Very walkable.* Possible to get by without a car.
- *50–70. Some walkable locations.* Some amenities in walking distance, but many everyday trips require a bike, public transport, or car.
- *25–50. Not walkable.* For most trips, public transport or a car is a must.
- *0–25. Driving only.* Virtually no destinations in walking range.

A high score means you can walk out your door and easily walk to shops, restaurants, or other services. Peter and Jennifer live in a place that is wonderful to take long wilderness walks in, but it would be quite a hike down to the grocery store. We try to bike instead for short runs to pick up a few things when we run out. But here's the real message: as you plan a move or a job change, check out the area for walkability. If you're selling your home, and convenience is an asset, let prospective buyers know about the walk score. It's a good example of how a green mindset affects your big decisions, not just your small ones.

Avoiding Throwaway

Okay, if the walk score influences your life's biggest decisions, like where you live and where you work, let's take a peek at some little choices where the green mindset brings better year-round results both at home and at work.

Holidays and parties are notorious for producing scrap beverage containers, cups, and utensils. All year round is a good time to stop drinking water in bottles and start toting around your own travel mug for coffee and water. Anne's son Alex's friend Elsa Marty now takes her own Tupperware to restaurants to pack up the leftovers instead of accepting those little pods. And

Anne has been reusing one plastic takeout clam at the office deli just so she can weigh her salad before taking it upstairs and putting it on a regular plate. Because Anne keeps a set of stoneware plates in her office, she can use them instead of throwaway stuff from the office parties. Give your office a set of plates, or have them buy one!

On her travels Anne took her own personal travel mug everywhere and used it for water too. She probably saved six or seven cups alone on her most recent business trip. That adds up.

And guess what—many churches are bringing back glass communion cups now. A young woman at our church dug them out of a closet and now leads the dishwashing crew on Sundays. No more plastic cups! Anne also brings a ceramic mug to coffee hour, formerly all Styrofoam. Others have followed her lead and now the coffee-hour ladies put out real mugs, too, so people can choose Styrofoam or ceramic. Again, it's a steady reduction in garbage and a changed habit with sustained consequences over the long run.

Front Yard Farmers

As food prices go higher and as we all become more aware of the environmental costs of growing, processing, and transporting food, more and more it's becoming time to take action on this front. Sure for Christmas, but also for all times of the year.

All across the country folks are getting their hands dirty and digging up their front or back yards to replace the water-hungry lawn with small food crops like lettuce, spinach, carrots, and corn. By giving up your high-maintenance lawn—it is estimated that nearly a third of all residential water goes toward lawns and ornamental gardens—and instead focusing on growing some of your own fruits and vegetables, you will be contributing in several ways: cutting back on water use, to be sure, but also helping to cleanse the air, reduce your own food bill, cut down on driving trips to pick up a few things for dinner, and meeting your neighbors by giving away the extra zucchini.

Jennifer and Peter have herbs, squash, lettuce, and tomatoes growing in their northern California front yard, and they help out in a community garden on their street that one neighbor with an unused side yard started. Anne grows tomatoes, rhubarb, chives, raspberries, and herbs in her Chicago back yard. Chances are you can grow something where you live too, even if it is just in containers on a porch.

The *Wall Street Journal* recently reported on the phenomenon of "front yard farmers." Front yard farmers piece together several nearby yards to make a small urban farm. A front yard farmer in Boulder, Colorado, farms on eight of his neighbors' yards, then gives the vegetables and herbs to the owners and has enough left to sell to nearby restaurants.

Front yard farming is an urban version of the Community Sustained Agriculture programs that deliver weekly boxes of veggies from small farms outside of cities. Could this work in your neighborhood? If you've always wanted to be a farmer, why not call together a few of your neighbors and pitch them the plan?

Not every neighbor or neighborhood is thrilled by this idea. Just like many homeowner's association rules have long banned hanging laundry (but are now overturning or reconsidering due to increased popular pressure from residents), not every neighborhood or city allows you to replace your carefully tended front lawn with something other than green grass. Check into the regulations first, and if they need to be modernized to fit our new world, take that task on too!

You can get information on small-scale farming from Spin-Farming LLC, a company that sells guides and holds seminars. SPIN stands for Small Plot Intensive, and they believe that their technique can help "create new farmland closer to metropolitan areas, which in turn will produce environmental, economic, and social benefits." Check them out at *www.spinfarming.com*.

Question Green Authority

Ah, you remember that old phrase, don't you? "Question authority." Has this green thing come full circle, back to its cradle in the sixties? Not exactly—we're talking about something a little different here.

"Question authority" means not always believing what seems to or portends to be "official." That part is still with us, and the same holds true with today's environmentalism. As you've read, countless big business and companies tout their green credentials in ads and marketing campaigns to cast their products in a greenish hue. But because something is marketed as green, should you buy it? Does that mean it is good? What it definitely means is that the company is paying close attention to trends and public opinion and wants to be on the consumer's good side.

I've Heard of Brainwashing and Whitewashing, But . . .

"Greenwashing" and "greenscamming" are on the rise as everyone claims to be green and to provide green products. You can visit *www.climatecounts.org* to get a scorecard on top U.S. corporations and their commitment to being green.

Wal-Mart regularly releases information on how quickly their customers have been embracing certain green products. The company's Live Better Index tracks five key purchase areas—compact fluorescent (CFL) light bulbs, concentrated/reduced packaging laundry detergent, extended-life paper products, organic baby food and formula, and organic milk. In spring 2008 they announced that purchases of these items were up 66 percent over the year before. The company now also plans to track sales of their shade-grown coffee and eco-friendly cleaning products. If Wal-Mart is going green, then green is definitely going mainstream!

On the other hand, a trendy frozen yogurt company was recently discovered to have fibbed a bit on their healthy, nonfat, and all-natural claim. Forced by a lawsuit to list the ingredients on their Web site, the company revealed a number of its products contained nonnatural ingredients.

Thankfully, we all seem to be looking at various green claims with a somewhat cautious and jaundiced eye. A survey by consulting firm WSL Strategic Retail turned up the fact that 42 percent of respondents were skeptical and don't trust that products labeled as "organic" actually are organic. Hopefully, over time, that will change.

So, eyes wide open, please, when evaluating the green and groovy claims of both big companies (who might surprise you by doing something right!) and small companies (who might surprise you by doing something less than right!).

In the Fast Lane: Is It Finally Time to Go Hybrid?

We've talked about choices, large and small. One of the larger choices you'll make, perhaps not this year but some time in the next five, ten, or fifteen, is on a new car. (Or a used one, if you're budget-conscious like Jennifer and Peter. Anne doesn't count because she doesn't have one at all!)

HYBRIDS AREN'T THE ONLY GREEN CARS
Don't think that you have to shell out $25–30,000 on a hybrid to get into the high-mpg game. Sure, hybrids are probably the best technology on the market today, but there are several "ordinary" vehicles on the market approaching 40 mpg or better—the Toyota Yaris, the Ford Focus, and the Honda Fit to name a few.

Hybrids are today's best way to deploy a promising technology toward reducing energy consumption and carbon footprints. Hybrids leapt in popularity in the past year, with registrations of newly purchased hybrids up a stunning 38 percent over 2006, and now command over 2 percent of the total car market. Part of the reason is rising energy prices, part is that an ever larger number of us are getting the green message, and part of it is that there are now so many more choices offered than when the hybrids first appeared.

Even large hybrid SUVs have started to show up—GM's Chevrolet Tahoe and the GMC Yukon both have hybrid versions. These heavy vehicles still don't get stellar mileage, but they do about 50 percent better than their gas-only equivalents. And except for the wildly popular Toyota Prius, the federal government is still offering generous tax credits (credits, not deductions, that's better) on most hybrid models. There are several sources of information; one of the best is the hybrid page at the EPA/Department of Energy's Fuel Economy site (*www.fueleconomy.gov/feg/tax_hybrid.shtml*).

Green by Example

How can you spread the green message? There is no point getting preachy with folks and scolding them for driving big SUVs and drinking their coffee out of Styrofoam cups. Not a way to win friends and influence people. Instead, make changes in your own life first, and then happily share the news about how great you think this is. Keep it focused on what you are doing right rather than on what you think they are doing wrong. Better to let them quietly examine their own lives and decide to make positive changes than to have you browbeat them into it.

Wrapping Up (Recyclable Wrap, of Course)

Can every moment of your Christmas be so intentional? No, but, overall, the holidays are a wonderful opportunity to live out your values. And if going green is emerging as a priority for you, it's a great time to start.

Is green a flash in the pan or a real opportunity for a change? We hope you agree it is an opportunity. We've spent time looking at the reasons and traditions of Christmas and trying to find a new way to see it. We hope we have given you many new ways you can create that tradition in your own little circle. Now it is time to sit back and watch the circles that your pebble creates move out and out and out.

DON'T FORGET WHO THIS PARTY WAS FOR

The true spirit of Christmas is the celebration of the birth of a man who taught love and set examples. Remember that.

Finally, we find that going green is about behavior, not just stuff and not just things you buy that have a green element to them. It's a mindset that influences your everyday decisions, not just a big decision about putting solar panels on your roof or not giving lavish Christmas gifts. It's not necessarily about doing less but about consciously choosing what to do instead of responding to relentless external forces. It is particularly about consuming less, it's about consuming smart, and it's about leaving smaller footprints at the other end of the consumption cycle. It's a gift that keeps on giving, and as we're coming to find out, one that will make you feel better and save you hard-earned "green" in the long run.

Let Christmas become the beginning of a new year of paying attention, of considering consequences, and of living smart.

Index